"A powerful and provocative book"

Dorie Clark, Author of *Reinventing You* and *Stand Out*.
Executive Education Faculty, Duke University
Fuqua School of Business

JUST ASK

Why Seeking Support is Your Greatest Strength

ANDY LOPATA

With additional research from a pilot study conducted by John Jameson

Just Ask

First published in 2020 by

Panoma Press Ltd
48 St Vincent Drive, St Albans, Herts, AL1 5SJ, UK
info@panomapress.com
www.panomapress.com

Book layout by Neil Coe.

978-1-784529-23-9

The right of Andy Lopata to be identified as the author of this work has been asserted in accordance with sections 77 and 78 of the Copyright, Designs and Patents Act 1988.

A CIP catalogue record for this book is available from the British Library.

This book is available online and in bookstores.

For Richard

And for anyone who feels alone and unable to ask for help.

Also for my Dad

Thank you for taking me on this journey.

"Judge a man by his questions rather than by his answers."

Voltaire

*"We might impress people with our strengths,
but we connect with people through our weaknesses."*

Craig Groeschel

*"Vulnerability is not weakness;
it's our greatest measure of courage."*

Brené Brown

What Others Say

"A powerful and provocative book that takes on one of the biggest challenges facing both business and individuals today. A combination of candid case studies, expert insight and practical tips makes this an essential read for anybody who needs to be more confident asking for help."

Dorie Clark, Author of *Reinventing You* and *Stand Out*. Executive Education Faculty, Duke University Fuqua School of Business

"I have spent my life developing incredible teams which go on to build exceptional companies. The invisible ingredient of the most successful companies is an extraordinary culture. But culture is not an abstract happening, it is the combined effort and shared spirit of people. Such alliance can only come about through communication and must be underwritten by trust.

In this book, Andy Lopata explains how authentic leaders understand that asking for help and revealing their true self establishes trust. Further, he explains how leaders can be strong and purposeful whilst still encouraging open dialogue.

Asking for support helps individuals and teams to overcome adversity. Teams where members are willing to ask for help achieve higher goals. Individuals achieve higher levels. Collaboration becomes the basis of growth and development.

I thoroughly recommend this book to anyone who wishes to lead, or to be part of, an extraordinary team and create a winning culture."

Kevin Gaskell, Ex-MD Porsche, BMW, Serial Entrepreneur, Corporate Trailblazer

"Too often, when we have an idea or a challenge, we are blinded by the accompanying emotions. We have our blinders on and aren't privy to the challenges and opportunities before us. As the book explains, gathering multiple perspectives is critical to enhancing our work.

Learning how to process the varying guidance is equally as important. Lopata's Review, Reframe, Respond framework is a useful and actionable model for seeking and processing guidance from others. It teaches how to tease out the useful information, pull apart other people's biases and leverage the feedback."

Ruth Gotian, EdD, MS

Chief Learning Officer in Anesthesiology

Former Assistant Dean for Mentoring and Executive Director of the Mentoring Academy

Weill Cornell Medicine

Forbes and Psychology Today contributor

"As someone who would give you their last dollar, but wouldn't ask you for a penny, this book really resonated with me. The strategies that Andy shares about how to ask for help are simple, pragmatic and powerful and I feel inspired to give them a try. This book is going to be a great help to many people who will now have the courage to ask for help, before it's too late."

Gordon Tredgold, Author of _F.A.S.T._, International Keynote Speaker on Leadership, Forbes Coach, Contributor and Columnist for Inc, Forbes, Entrepreneur, Fortune and CEO World.

"This book should be required reading in the boardrooms of UK PLC and beyond. It is both thought-provoking and surprising.

Andy argues we have to stop lying every day responding to the question 'How are you?' with 'I'm fine'. Often, we are not fine and actually could do with some help, but few ask because they perceive it as a sign of weakness.

Yet this ability to ask, says Andy, is vital for a healthy office culture and case histories he has gathered from around the world underline this, showing a trend towards compassion in business.

These are extraordinary times in which to live and thrive but Andy thinks people are beginning to realise they need to start being open and vulnerable. This book definitely proves you need to 'Just Ask'."

Lady Val Corbett, Founder of Lady Val's Professional Women's Network, The Corbett Network and Robin Corbett Award.

"Andy has done a brilliant job of making this difficult topic real through stories. He both normalises the extent of and variety of mental health challenges and then sets out a toolbox to start the journey of moving forward. All in an easy read too!"

Perry Burton, Head of People and Culture, Grant Thornton UK

"Entrepreneurs are under a lot of pressure to perform – often they encounter stress, complexity and difficult choices. For many entrepreneurs, they struggle to know who to talk to for support and camaraderie as they face these challenges. Sometimes they share too much publicly and damage their brand. Sometimes they bottle things up too much and it weighs them down.

This book explores the right way to ask for help so you can rebound feeling better and stronger than ever. You might also find you make deeper connections and lifelong friendships with trusted peers who go through business and life challenges together."

**Daniel Priestley, Author of *Entrepreneur Revolution*,
Cofounder of Dent Global**

"Andy's pragmatic and no-nonsense writing is refreshing to read. He challenges some of the thinking that has become the norm in society and encourages us to look at life through a different lens. A worthwhile read with lots of useful considerations."

Jack Ismail, Partnership Director, Specsavers UK & ROI

"This book could quite easily have been speaking about me.

It's the mirror so many of us have been holding up for so many years. Don't show your vulnerable side, it's career limiting. Don't trust anyone. Throughout our careers we are told lots of 'don'ts'.

Things have got to change; the world has changed. During the early part of 2020 and Covid-19, I lost four family members in one hit. I had no choice but to reach out to my genuine friends in my huge network, who couldn't wait to provide me with virtual hugs, love and support. Andy was one of them.

So a very timely read for us all and to share with our family and friends. As Covid-19 swept into our lives like a tornado, it was also a timely reminder that we should let others in to help in the way that we are always helping others.

Congratulations Andy, for being brave, authentic and just the beautiful way you have articulated this message for us all to see the value of networks and friendships."

Dr Heather Melville OBE CCMI, Director,
People Networks & Client Relationship Programmes, PwC

"In this book, Andy Lopata empowers the reader by demonstrating the art of asking for help and how it could be a powerful strategy for a successful leader and entrepreneur. Andy addresses how asking for help is not a weakness from different perspectives.

Having read this, I now feel confident asking for help, which I didn't before. *Just Ask* provides a mind shift for any leader and the knowledge to use it for better outcomes."

Shaikha Al Rahoomi,

Director of Strategic Planning Division,

Executive & Life Coach,

Board member of Emirates Strategic Planning and Future Foresight Association

"The world of work and how we as individuals interact is ever changing and never more so than in the past 12 months. In this new book, Andy Lopata helps the reader explore vulnerability, team work, sharing and seeking help. An easy to digest format with compelling stories to help the reader grow and develop. In my opinion a must read."

Michael Strawbridge,

Global Head of Content, Networks and Member Services,

The Learning & Performance Institute

"*Just Ask* is the antithesis of a 'self-help' book but is rather a clarion call that we need to have both the courage *and* the strategy to ask for help and develop the capacity for others to do the same.

Where this book differs from conventional books is that the author role models his message by sharing his own story with vulnerability, among the other diverse and inspiring stories. This brings his important message to life.

When someone asks 'How are you?' your reply will never be the same again.

Highly recommended."

Steven D'Souza, Head of Executive Development, Bestselling Author, Leadership Consultant and Coach

"I found *Just Ask* full of insights and strategies, but most interesting for me were the real-life stories of so many people in different walks of life who had each benefitted from eventually asking for help.

I wish I had been handed a copy of *Just Ask* 30 years ago. Well done Andy for creating something that everyone should read."

Richard McCann, Times No1 Bestselling Author of *Just a Boy*

"Andy Lopata's new book *Just Ask* is a revelation!

Andy has created something which all of us absolutely need to read. This inspiring book has a fundamental message for us all: share how we really feel and don't be afraid to ask for help when we need it. While global leaders demonstrate macho attitudes to solving problems, Andy reminds us our ultimate strength lies in allowing ourselves to display vulnerability and demonstrating authenticity. *Just Ask* allows us to become our own role models.

This book is an inspiring read. It motivates us all to take the plunge while providing an invaluable roadmap on how to reach out for help and in so doing, be an inspiration to others.

Seeking support truly is our greatest strength.

I loved it!"

John Stapleton, Co-Founder, New Covent Garden Soup Company

"Insightful, powerful, relevant book about understanding the change in mindset and courage needed today to fully appreciate and embrace the power of our networks. A must read."

Charles Marcus,
President of The Empowerment International Group Inc.
Ranked as one of the "Top 60 Motivational Speakers in the World"
by hunger2succeed

Contents

Prologue

This book begins with a dedication to Richard. Let me explain why.

In late March 2016 I heard the news that Richard had died suddenly. He had always been a fit and healthy man and no more information was offered.

Richard was one of the nicest men you could ever wish to meet. Known to family and friends as a 'gentle giant', he always wore a warm smile and was generous with his time and willing to help and support people in his network. He actively strived to make a difference to the people around him in his life.

As we waited for news of the funeral, many of Richard's mutual friends exchanged shocked condolences and sought an answer. Nobody seemed to know what had happened. Richard was cremated in mid-April, a few weeks after his death. I couldn't attend unfortunately but was told by several people that there was standing room only at the church.

A week later over 50 people travelled to Richard's hometown for a walk in the surrounding hills (something that Richard loved during his life) followed by a memorial lunch.

Over half the people there took the opportunity to share a memory of the friend we had lost, and each of them told stories that had a common thread. Richard was one of life's givers. He was always there for his network and friends and his attention would always be on what he could do for others, not on what they could do for him.

One mourner had flown in from Africa and she shared how Richard had travelled at his own cost for a week to help her to set up a charity in her native country.

Another flew into this small English village from the US just to pay his respects. He said something that was later to have huge resonance.

"You know what," he started, "I still don't know what Richard did for a living. Every time we met he was only interested in me, in what I was doing and how he could help. He never talked about himself."

The next day I found out what had happened. My worst suspicions were confirmed. Richard had taken his own life.

His wife, Caroline, told me, "Richard was helping many people but wasn't necessarily using his ability to develop the business that he strived for. You see, helping others to do what they strived to do and teaching them to do that was the way that he should have made a living. Giving was more important to him but that philosophy was to some extent his downfall.

"The fact that he helped others but didn't leverage that gift to generate an income meant that he suffered financial difficulties. Those difficulties contributed greatly to his ultimate decision to take his own life."

It's a twisted irony that, when it mattered, Richard wasn't able to allow that same network to help him. And I have no doubt that the people at his memorial lunch, those at his funeral and many others who couldn't be at either would have had no hesitation in helping in any way they could.

Caroline ended her eulogy at Richard's funeral by saying, "There are many memories to treasure, Richard was a unique and much-loved gentle giant with a very big heart, he will always be remembered with a smile."

There was a lot of love for Richard in that room and, I'm sure, enough resource, both financial and emotional, to have ensured that he could have got back on his feet.

I'm not saying that Richard was wrong or at fault for not sharing his woes with his network. That oversimplifies a very difficult and complex situation and he sadly wasn't the first person to have chosen this drastic route rather than open up to people and let them help him. And he won't be the last.

So many things stop us from asking for help. What we don't always realise is that people want to help, they like to help and they will feel hurt if we don't let them help.

So many things stop us from asking for help. What we don't always realise is that people want to help, they like to help and they will feel hurt if we don't let them help.

Everyone at Richard's funeral and memorial lunch was hurting.

I believe that the world was changing dramatically, even before Covid-19 and the global lockdown that made us more aware of our own vulnerability, that of people around us and the need to ask for help.

Not least, we are moving away from an insular, macho attitude that is mired in the last century where we were judged on our strengths and ability to solve our own issues. An attitude that didn't discriminate; it impacted all of us, irrespective of gender or personality type. Richard certainly wasn't an 'alpha male' yet still he felt unable to share what was happening and ask for support.

We are moving towards a world where it's OK to share, OK to not know all of the answers. We are moving towards a world where 'vulnerability' is no longer a dirty word and where 'authenticity' is a buzzword.

But we're not moving fast enough.

About This Book

What's Holding Us Back?

As a society I believe that we are too slow to ask for help. The vast majority of us are brought up to believe that we need to know all of the answers, find solutions independently and look good. The rise of social media and the Instagram and Snapchat-fuelled selfie culture has compounded that belief, driving an obsession with creating the perfect look and the perfect life for our online followers.

It's not just about online interactions with relative strangers though. How often do you truly open up and be honest with your friends and family when asked how you are?

How often do you truly open up and be honest with your friends and family when asked how you are?

A decade or two ago we were overwhelmed by self-help gurus telling us to stop responding to the question 'How are you?' by simply saying 'I'm OK' or 'Fine thanks'. Instead, they told us to be positive. Suddenly everyone was saying 'I'm brilliant', 'I'm fantastic', 'I'm great', with a broad toothy grin that often hid a very different truth.

I noticed something similar within the professional community. I've been lucky enough to be a member of the Professional

Speaking Association (PSA) in the UK since 2003. The people I have met through the PSA are more than competitors, associates and colleagues; many of them are my friends. We call each other 'our tribe' and we mean it.

Yet even though we identify as friends, we are still not honest enough with each other. When we meet and catch up at regional meetings and conferences, behind the pleasure of seeing our friends we still want to shine. The same drive to look good is prevalent within a community of people who enjoy supporting each other.

So, when people ask us 'How's business?' we reply 'It's fantastic', 'It's great', 'I'm so busy'.

But we don't always mean it.

I remember attending a regional PSA event a few years ago. One of the speakers was Steven Houghton-Burnett, who made a fortune by starting, growing and selling one of the UK's first internet service providers and went on to be an excellent business and motivational speaker.

Steven was running a workshop that day and handed every delegate a questionnaire to complete at the beginning of his session.

One of the questions was: 'What stage is your business at in its development?'

A. Brand new (less than six months old)

B. Young (less than two years old)

C. Mature and stable

D. Growing

E. In decline

Not one person in the group was prepared to admit that their business was in decline. Everybody had a business that was either in its early stages, mature and stable or growing.

There were liars in that room. I know that there were liars in that room. I was lying! At that stage my business was in the middle of a slump. It was definitely 'in decline'. But I didn't feel comfortable owning up to that fact at that time and with that group. I'm sure I wasn't the only one in that room pretending that their business was stronger than it really was.

The need to look good can often stop us from sharing, even with our closest family, friends and colleagues. We want them to think the best of us and that need overrides the possibility of getting support or advice that might change our situation, or at least make it more bearable.

The need to look good stops us from sharing. We want people to think the best of us and that need overrides the possibility of getting support or advice that might change our situation.

Prince William and Prince Harry have spoken out a lot about the 'toxic masculinity' that prevents people from sharing, particularly young men. In a 2017 interview, The Duke of Cambridge said, "For too long there has been a taboo about talking about some important issues. If you were anxious, it's because you were weak. If you couldn't cope with whatever life threw at you, it's because you were failing. Successful, strong people don't suffer like that, do they? But of course, we all do. It's just that few of us speak about it"[1].

Myth Busting

I believe that people are now ready to see these myths busted and create a new world view. One where it is not only OK to be open, honest and vulnerable but also where it's positively encouraged. The success of Brené Brown's books and TED Talks[2] on the power of vulnerability and the willingness of big business to embrace the message suggests that we're more receptive to the need to change our approach than ever before.

It's important for individuals to know that it's OK to acknowledge what we feel, what challenges us and what is holding us back. You don't need to be positive all of the time.

You don't need to be positive all of the time.

Hippo Time

It's OK to be negative occasionally too. In Paul McGee's excellent book *S.U.M.O. (Shut Up Move On)*[3] he talks about the importance of 'Hippo Time'. McGee explains that one of his friends told him that he didn't want to 'move on', as the book encourages when something goes wrong, he just wanted to wallow.

"None of us want to hear some well-meaning person telling us to cheer up when we've just experienced a major setback or disappointment," said his friend. "Telling someone to SUMO might in some circumstances be both insensitive and unhelpful, particularly if what they have experienced is serious and significant."

McGee explained, "When Steve used the term wallow, a picture of a hippopotamus wallowing in mud immediately sprang to mind. It was then that I realised that on occasions, before people can SUMO they may need to wallow – to have, as I call it, some *Hippo Time*."

I love this concept of 'Hippo Time' and confess to wallowing myself on occasion. My objective in this book is to encourage you to be more open with your network. But timing is key and if you need time out first in order to process your feelings, move through the stages of frustration or grief and clear your head, then that's fine. The important thing is not to wallow for too long, otherwise the negative feelings will start to take over and control your actions and responses.

I want you to feel that it's OK to share. To recognise that constantly being independent and self-sufficient is counterproductive. Pretending that you know all the answers doesn't serve anyone. It damages your morale and confidence; it means you repeat mistakes that others have already made and learned from; and it leads to inefficiency that costs you and the people around you.

Vulnerability doesn't need to be framed as a sign of weakness. Saying 'I don't know' doesn't mean you're not a star performer, high achiever or ambitious. Changing your mind or admitting your mistakes shouldn't indicate weakness. It's a strength and, in fact, humility is becoming increasingly important as a business skill.

People do want to help you. We enjoy helping people we care about.

Like everything there is 'a time and a place'. It has become clear in the interviews I've carried out for the book that there are times when it's definitely not appropriate to share. For the Premiership footballer, voicing doubts and a lack of confidence can mean the loss of their place in the team and their livelihood. For the New

Zealand marine it can be the difference between the rest of their squad relying on them and feeling secure in combat or not.

You can, however, create a strategy for sharing:

- Build a strong network of trusted contacts in whom you are comfortable confiding and with whom you are happy sharing.

- Have clarity about where in your life or career you need support and the people you'd be happy to turn to.

- Develop deep relationships with key people who will meet with you regularly, listen to your challenges, explore them with you, help you find solutions and hold you accountable for your actions.

When we hide in the shadows hoping that our anonymity will preserve our reputation, we don't allow that help to flourish. Without the support of others we're far more likely to fail. Help and support are all around us: all we need to do is ask.

The Just Ask Journey

It finally came together in a dream.

After months of frustration, high emotion and near despair, the elusive structure of this book came to me in a dream at about 3 o'clock in the morning on the Saturday before Christmas. And, appropriately, it was the unwitting help of two of my professional colleagues that brought it all together.

I dreamed that I finally found the right format for this book by collaborating with my colleagues, each of us taking one key area to focus on. Why those two colleagues I don't know. I hadn't actually spoken to them about the book and their expertise as represented in the dream didn't reflect their expertise in real life. But that didn't matter.

I woke up with a start, scrambling to remember the details of the dream. I knew the answer was there. I knew that I was writing about courage – the courage to ask for help. I knew that the sections my colleagues were writing were planning and taking action. For the next three hours I sat in bed writing up a new chapter plan, bringing the themes in the previous manuscript into line with the new structure, before collapsing into a weary sleep around 6am.

But how did it come to this, over three years since the start of this project and nearly a year after the original manuscript had been completed?

Not Good Enough

Just five weeks earlier I had stood on stage at Ambition 2019, a conference I help to organise every year to support charities in my local area, and delivered my 'Just Ask' talk for the third time.

Originally this had been planned to be part of my launch campaign, a chance to celebrate the publication of the book with my local business community. We had even arranged with the key sponsor the purchase of a copy of the book for each delegate.

But I had no book to deliver.

Two weeks beforehand my publisher had emailed me to tell me that they didn't believe in the latest manuscript, the third draft of the book, and recommended that we agree to tear up our contract. This represented a huge setback to me. Not just to my dreams of seeing this book published but also, it felt, to my reputation. I had agreed a contract with one of the best known publishers in the world, celebrated it publicly and now they were declaring that I was not good enough.

I hadn't told anyone. I was well aware of the irony of not telling my network about this huge setback when it related to a book about transparency, vulnerability and asking for help. But I needed my Hippo Time. I didn't know whether I would share what was happening with the book in my talk but I knew it was a possibility. It was too raw to plan. However, as I came towards the end of my presentation, I knew that it felt right.

The response from the people at that conference was incredible. So many people came up to me and urged me to carry on and offering support. I even had the offer of an introduction to a new potential publisher the next day.

I needed that boost. I knew that this was an important book for me to complete and get out there but the frustration had been building up for months and I couldn't see a clear way ahead. I needed other people to confirm that my instinct was right.

I needed other people to confirm that my instinct was right.

Life Imitating Advice

My journey of writing *Just Ask* reflects much of the advice offered within its pages. Some books are easy to write and come together naturally. This hasn't been one of those books.

The feedback from my publisher wasn't the first time that they had been unhappy with the manuscript. The first was way too long, which I knew and accepted, and the second wasn't deemed a fit either. The second rejection really impacted me. I didn't agree with the feedback and my initial response was anger. I had worked so hard on this book and was so attached to it that brutal critique of the end product wasn't well received.

But after a period of stewing and then reflection, I realised that I was far too close to be objective. I decided to follow my own advice and just ask. I reached out to a few people in my network who I really trust. Among them accomplished authors of highly respected and successful books and senior leaders in the corporate world.

A couple of people loved the book and, of course, I wanted to latch on to that feedback.

However, there was a common theme from a few more that I forced myself to listen to. As one reviewer put it, "You have a brilliant book here Andy but this isn't it."

It was back to the drawing board. I went away to the mountains in Ireland and I restructured the book. Again, I went to more people in my network for their objective feedback and again the message was that the book wasn't quite right. I knew it needed to be restructured but didn't know how. I felt lost – until my dream.

Still, I asked for help. I reached out to a good friend and one of my reviewers, David McQueen, and asked for his time. He very generously gave me his time and attention and we went through the manuscript and brought the existing content into the new structure. Now, with a new publisher, the book finally sees the light of day.

From day one of this project, when I posted my intention to write this book on social media, I have turned to my network for help and support. It might be my name on the cover but it's definitely been a team effort. Even in my dream it was others who came to my rescue!

I've had plenty of moments of frustration, anxiety, anger and desperation. Ultimately though, the book has been published and you are reading it and there's one simple reason for that.

I was always willing to open up, be vulnerable and just ask.

SECTION ONE
FINDING THE COURAGE

1.

Processing Your Emotions

One of the biggest challenges for me in the journey of writing this book, as shared in the previous chapter, has been managing my emotions throughout the process. There have been times where I wanted to just publish what I had, even if it meant walking away from a prestigious contract, and others where I even felt like giving up entirely.

My book journey is just a microcosm of life as a whole. All of this happened during a period where my business was struggling (given the number of hours invested in interviews, research and writing, the two challenges may not be completely unrelated). Meanwhile the strongest temptation was to internalise all of the pain and keep projecting a successful image to the world.

Are things any different for you? Whether in your job or your day-to-day life, how many challenges are you faced with that peck at your ego, make you question your abilities and right to be who the world thinks you to be?

How many challenges are you faced with every day that peck at your ego, make you question your abilities and right to be who the world thinks you to be?

How often do you want to lash out at your boss, or your team? Feel lost and unable to perform or wait for people to praise or reassure you but not feel able to ask directly?

My objective in writing this book is to encourage you to share these emotions more readily. As wonderful as it would be for you to put the book down and simply start sharing, life doesn't work like that. Despite focusing on this topic for the last four years, I still had to recognise when I wasn't asking for help and force myself to do so on more than one occasion. And the chances are that, as you are reading these lines, I'm going through the same emotions yet again.

Very few of us find it natural to be vulnerable and ask for help. Years of conditioning mean that we are driven by a number of fears and emotions that actively prevent us from doing so. There is a process that we need to go through before we are able to ask and it starts with finding the courage.

Make Some Space

Paul McGee's concept of Hippo Time has been central to my coping with the challenges I shared in the previous chapter. As I explained, when the third manuscript was turned down, for two weeks I told no one. I simply raged. And I needed to do that.

I needed to create the space to think more clearly. Once the emotions had run their course, I felt far more able to take the right steps. And, interestingly, I was able to listen objectively to feedback, take it in my stride and positively decide on the right course of action.

It's not always possible, or even desirable, to open up immediately about everything that is bothering us. If we don't allow ourselves the space to process our emotions, we don't allow ourselves the opportunity to be objective when seeking advice. And we lack clarity going forward as a result.

If we don't allow ourselves the space to process our emotions, we don't allow ourselves the opportunity to be objective when seeking advice.

However, there is a balance. And we need to ensure that we limit our Hippo Time before our wallowing becomes deeply entrenched and therefore counterproductive.

When you feel the rage or despair rising, listen to yourself and your thoughts and set aside a time to begin to share and to ask for help. Feel free to stand still for a while but keep your eye on a point where you know you have to start moving forward.

Billy the Boxer

One person who let the rage and despair take over was former World Light-welterweight Boxing Champion Billy Schwer. When Billy lost his hard-won world title after a bruising 11-round battle with Argentinean Pablo Sarmiento in July 2001, his life went off the rails.

"My whole life I had been Billy the Boxer. Now I was just Billy. I did not know who Billy was," he told me. "The end of the road for me was when I was in hospital once I lost the world title. There was no way back from there, it was different. I went through a really tough time. I went through an identity crisis. I really struggled.

"I could not see a future for myself outside of a boxing ring. I was lost and I felt alone and empty. I had nothing to get out of bed for. I had been a world-class athlete, a world-class champion, so now what?"

Billy describes the next two years as the worst of his life. He struggled with depression, his marriage fell apart, he went bankrupt and he found himself considering suicide. From being on top of the world he had plummeted to rock bottom.

"I would not listen to anyone. I was so pig-ignorant, so single-minded, so selfish. Those are the attributes that helped me become a world champion but the paradox is the things that helped me become a champion in the ring were helping me fail outside.

"I didn't know how to be anything other than Billy the Boxer. I was trained and conditioned to fight and attack, defend and resist, from eight years of age. That is who I was, that is who I thought I was."

A chance meeting with an old friend rescued Billy from his descent and would ultimately help change the trajectory of his life.

Reinventing Billy

Soon after he lost his title his friend had told him about a self-development programme. The Landmark Forum[4] completely changed Billy.

"It was only when I did the Landmark Forum that I started to unveil other parts of myself. I have still got that fight in me but it is not who I am. There is so much more to me. I did not know that at that time, as a 31-year-old. Billy the Boxer had me survive and get me to where I was at that point. But at that point Billy the Boxer was redundant."

The Landmark Forum is a challenging environment. Participants are encouraged to share openly and honestly, revealing their deepest fears and insecurities, peeling the layers away from their lives and identifying the events that shaped them. I wondered how Billy the Boxer, a very single-minded entity, used to punching back in the ring, handled the process.

"It took me three days of getting battered. I was hammered and I loved it because I love a fight. It was taking me somewhere I had never been before.

"I now know that after that last time in the ring I made an unconscious decision that my life was over. To somebody who thinks that their life is over, you just do not care. I went off the rails. After Landmark I took the responsibility of getting back in control of my life and being responsible for my future and I pulled myself back together. I was losing the game; I was losing life.

"Then I looked back. I had been top of the bill in Las Vegas. I had enjoyed an extraordinary career. I had an extraordinary life. Yet I knew there was something else if I wanted. When you're in that place you have to be willing to find the courage to go to work and have a look. You have to break the habit of being yourself."

Talking to Ourselves

I took the Landmark programme myself a few years ago and one of the most important lessons I learned from that experience was the power we have to tell ourselves a story. We all have an inner voice, the Landmark programme calls them 'rackets', which tell us what we can and can't do.

It's these rackets, formed from a lifetime of creating stories about our lives based on our experiences and what others say to us, that can get in the way of opening up and asking for the help that we need.

It's these rackets that can get in the way of opening up and asking for the help that we need.

We tell ourselves that we'll look foolish if we share our challenges, that other people don't want, or won't be able, to help us or that they won't trust or respect us anymore.

But how often is our perception accurate? Time and again people are pleasantly surprised when they ask for help and others leap to their support. Ultimately, we like to help other people but we don't allow others to help us – because of the voices in our head.

Think Like a Four-Year-Old

It's easy to see rock stars perform effortlessly night after night in front of tens of thousands of people and figure that it's easy for them. The world of self-doubt, of nerves and anxiety is not one they seem to inhabit. But that would be far from the truth.

By 2010 Hattie Webb and her sister Charley had been touring as backing singers with legendary Canadian singer Leonard Cohen for two years. At a concert in Odense, Denmark, in front of about 20,000 people, Hattie fainted.

"Touring is extraordinary and very strenuous," Hattie told me. "On tour with Leonard, the shows were four hours each night, often in quite challenging environments. It demands a lot of energy from everyone involved and I had fainted during a show and hit my head."

Hattie was OK. She got up and carried on with the concert. But the incident affected her going forward. Hattie found that she developed an anxiety of fainting that she later identified as a fear of failure.

She underwent a lot of coaching and therapy to resolve it. She reviewed how she was living her life and how she was treating herself but she also examined how her internal dialogue was affecting her.

"All of us isolate; we all have negative thoughts, that's natural. It's not whether or not you have negative thoughts, it's what you do with them. The anxiety was suddenly very present.

All of us isolate; we all have negative thoughts, that's natural. It's not whether or not you have negative thoughts, it's what you do with them.

"When I look back there were signs that I could have made changes earlier. If you don't listen to your body, the voice gets louder, the symptoms get more intense and the anxiety increases."

Hattie believes that she is often very hard on herself and that was the cause of much of her anxiety. Learning to stop and accept that other factors can influence outcomes and, if necessary, asking others to help, has been a key factor in helping her to recover her confidence and composure.

"I often see when you are hard on yourself that it's not necessarily just from your own mind, it's how you have been taught to be with yourself by teachers and people in positions of authority. It's not anyone's fault, but to actually claim how you want to treat yourself moving forward is very empowering.

"There is a wonderful meditation which Louise Hay, the founder of Hay House Publishing, encourages. She asks you to imagine yourself as a four-year-old; if you have any four-year-olds in your life you know that if they do something wrong or if they fall over or if they spill something, you try and say, 'Oh don't worry' or 'That's OK' or 'Let me help you'.

"So, you use that kind of dialogue with yourself, particularly when something goes wrong. You're not shouting at yourself on the inside. You are actually treating yourself kindly, it makes a huge difference."

I suggested to Hattie that such an approach would make it easier for you to let other people help because if you're being easier on yourself then you're going to be more open to finding resolution and stop worrying about looking bad.

Hattie agreed. "That's so true; being a fortress means that it is more difficult to share easily. It's so important to know your worth and be open and flexible to being vulnerable. I always think that being vulnerable takes strength. It's not a weakness."

Being a fortress means that it is more difficult to share easily.

Don't Procrastinate

Building up the courage to ask for help means having an understanding of what holds us back in the first place. Being able to recognise your inner voice and challenge it is the first step. And yes, you may need to take some time to process those emotions and thoughts before moving forward.

But don't let it hold you back for too long. It is easy to procrastinate, putting off the key conversations because of everything that might go wrong. After all, if we don't take risks then what have we got to lose?

The answer is everything. The solutions to your challenges live in the world around you. The people who trust you and who like and love you have probably been through something similar – it is amazing how often you find that you're not alone after all.

We all feel alone with our fears and vulnerability at times yet in truth that's not necessarily the case. But if we procrastinate, holding back those fears and not expressing them, then we can't identify the people around us who share the same challenges or who might have the great ideas to help us to overcome them.

We all need our Hippo Time. We need to process our emotions and understand what we need to share and with whom. And then we need to take that leap into the unknown and ask for help.

2.

LOOKING GOOD

Pegine Echevarria was brought up in a Puerto Rican community in the Bronx. They weren't among the poorest communities in New York but they were very close. Pegine's father was an alcoholic who could never hold down a job. The family moved home 20 times in the first 12 years of her life as he always struggled to make the rent.

By the age of 13 the turmoil in Pegine's family had produced a vulnerable, angry, stubborn young woman lacking in direction and confidence.

"My middle school had about 3,000 kids," Pegine explained, "and I learned early on that people don't deal with crazy people, they get too afraid. So, I would walk up these big stairs, to the first level, and I would sing the song from *Annie*, 'The Sun Will Come Out Tomorrow!'. I would sing and everyone would go, 'That girl is whack'.

"Then the next day I would go back and I would scream, 'What's your problem?! Are you gonna start with me?!' I knew if they thought I was crazy I would stay out of trouble."

Pegine's bravado led to an invitation to join one of the many gangs being formed in the neighbourhood. Her reputation as someone who was 'crazy' protected her, even from running the gauntlet usually required before joining the gang. She dressed the part as well: "My jackets had chains, real bike chains, because you could take them out and whip them up."

The look and the gang gave Pegine something that she had never felt before: a sense of protection, pride and belonging. "None of us had ever felt that we were good enough, had ever thought that we were smart enough. We were told that we were losers, each one of us in our own way."

Pegine's protective façade was driven by a need to look good and be part of something. Showing any vulnerability would only expose her to danger; the look, the gang and her reputation protected her from the outside world and no one would be able to get in.

La Loca, the nickname given to her by the gang, was a tough act to maintain but it was important that she was seen as strong, dangerous and inviolable on the streets. But there needed to be an outlet for the fear and doubt that naturally hid behind the mask.

From a young age Pegine was an avid journal writer, keeping a diary and writing letters to herself. "I would write and write pages, crying and writing and having angry conversations with God. I wrote letters to me and I wrote letters to my future kids.

"I kept them all. You can see that I was crying because you could see the tears on the page.

"I didn't talk to people because I thought I was the only one that was living that life; I sure as hell didn't talk to my fellow gang members. I had a lot of emotion to release and I did that through the pages of the journal."

Scouting for Girls

Pegine's mother eventually became aware of the situation her daughter found herself in and, desperate not to see her daughter go off the rails, called the Girl Scouts to see what they could do.

So it was that Pegine found herself in a programme for troublemakers led by a Wall Street banker who wanted to make a difference. When she turned up on her first day Pegine insisted on wearing her gang jacket. Two girls from other gangs also turned up similarly attired, the need to look good still reigned supreme.

"In walked Miss B. She said, 'Girls, you are in my program. We are not going to sell cookies, we are not going to be doing arts and crafts. I am going to take you downtown and I am going to show you what a tough woman really looks like. The only rule is you have to wear the hat.'

"Every Wednesday afternoon we would go down to Manhattan; three girls with really long hair, with gang jackets and Girl Scout hats. Miss B would stop women in the street who looked professional and go, 'Tell these girls how you got to where you are, because you're a fighter, aren't you?' The women would agree but I did notice how they would hold on to their pocketbooks a little tighter.

"She helped us see that we could shift this tough angry persona, that we could be tough, confident and strong in this other world."

Joining the Girl Scouts became the first major turning point. Pegine would go on to become a very successful businesswoman and television personality in the United States.

The façade of looking good remained. Pegine and her fellow gang members still insisted on retaining their gang identities but she started to see that there was a route out of the hole she had dug for herself.

Not looking good is probably the biggest fear that prevents most of us from asking for help and support. We all wear our own versions of Pegine's gang jacket and chains. We all have our own moments where we stand at the top of a staircase and sing songs from *Annie* and then go home and cry into our diaries.

Of course, I mean that metaphorically – in most cases anyway. But the modern equivalent are the Instagram selfies and motivational quotes or Facebook status updates that tell the world that we are invincible and on top of it all.

We would much rather be seen to look good and suffer in silence than be seen to be vulnerable.

We would much rather be seen to look good and suffer in silence than be seen to be vulnerable.

As Pegine moved away from the streets and towards a successful career in business, she learned the power and importance of honesty, openness and authenticity.

"To this day I know that being vulnerable, being open to sharing me… my feelings, thoughts and experiences, is my power. I chose not to lie about who I am, what I feel and how I think. Being vulnerable, I have learned, makes me relatable, connected, responsive and authentic. My opening up my heart, which is really scary for most, has been my salvation and super power."

What Other People Think

The belief that we have to look good in front of others is founded on a series of stories that we create for ourselves. We develop a narrative in our own minds of how people will respond and what they will think and say if we open up and tell them exactly what we think or feel.

But all too often these are stories, not reality. How many times have you been surprised at a positive reaction to something you have built yourself up to confess to your nearest and dearest? I'm not saying that the stories we create are always wrong but they are certainly not always right and often based on fear. And we often don't find out the reality because the fiction prevents us from taking action.

I believe that our concern about how other people see and judge us is the number one factor that prevents us from being truly authentic in the way we live our lives. And the sad irony is that we're all walking around wearing masks and acting out a charade, hiding from each other the fact that we share similar concerns, similar fears and similar vulnerabilities.

Our concern about how other people see and judge us is the number one factor that prevents us from being truly authentic in the way we live our lives.

A friend of mine who supports the same football team as me offers a prime example. Always seen with a smile on his face, enjoying life and the centre of the social scene at home and away games, it was a shock to hear that he had tried to take his own life. But he has since found that many of the men attending the same matches, conforming to the terrace stereotype, put on a brave 'alpha' face among their friends but in the background also suffer from depression and self-doubt.

Among any group of 'lads' attending sporting events around the world there are likely to be a number of people whose relationships are in trouble, who are not happy in their jobs, who face financial difficulties or who are plagued by a range of similar challenges. Yet you wouldn't recognise that when you see them drinking, singing, laughing and cheering together. They are the human equivalent of peacocks showing off their tail feathers. Particularly in the macho environment around sports, it's unlikely that you will see them admit vulnerability. Everyone has to look good.

Maybe that moment of escapism, where sport and friendship provide relief from the day-to-day, is not the time to focus on those issues. But what if we did drop the mask? What if that group of lads took advantage of the hours spent in each other's company to share what's holding them back and causing them grief? How powerful would it be for them to find out that others in the group are going through the same thing?

Occasionally sad events like my friend's attempted suicide shift the conversation, just for a moment before the alpha pattern reasserts itself. But ultimately this is a prime example of the need to look good in a group overriding the potential of sharing and opening up.

Wearing a Mask

Worrying about what other people think can even lead to us living a false life, pretending to be someone we're not.

In 1992, when Jerome Joseph was a teenager, he was attacked by a group of ten men who were harassing the three female friends he was with. Trying to protect the girls but outnumbered, Jerome was savagely beaten up. He was initially hit from behind and then kicked and stamped on as he hit the floor.

"I got up," Jerome explained, "with the adrenaline of the fight still pumping in my veins, and I made my way to the window of a shop. I looked at my reflection, peering at my state.

"The first thing that came into my mind was 'my rainbow shirt is torn'. I spent all my pocket money on it and I was upset to see it torn in multiple places. But that was not the only thing; my face was the size of a watermelon.

"The girls came running back as I was peering in the mirror; I turned around and asked them, 'Can you see if anything is torn on this shirt?' That was when they started screaming.

I was confused. How bad was the tear in the shirt? I turned my head and it was then I saw a knife sticking out of my back."

Jerome was stabbed 15 times, one wound missing his heart by an inch and his lung was punctured. While he still has a physical scar from the attack, the real impact was psychological. And not from the attack itself but from the response of his community to what had happened.

Jerome explained, "Family, friends and community started to avoid me because no one wanted to mix with a guy who got stabbed. Remember that this was the 90s and traditional word of mouth was all we had at that point. The word on the street was that I was a bad guy who got into fights.

"I still remember one moment vividly. I went to a community event and there were kids playing. As I was playing with them their mothers came over and quickly pulled their children away. They didn't want their kids to mix with a guy who just got stabbed, the bad guy. I was devastated. I felt like I let my family down. My family who were proud members of the community now had to face the shame of what I had done."

Driven by that shame, Jerome told his parents that they would never talk of the attack again and would simply pretend it hadn't happened. They agreed that hiding the attack would be best for his life, his career and how others saw him.

"As a result, I took this box and I took the pain, the fear, and I locked it up there, hidden in a corner. And I told myself this did not happen. It never happened. Forget it and the shame will go away."

I took this box and I took the pain, the fear, and I locked it up there, hidden in a corner. And I told myself this did not happen.

Jerome kept his story locked away for 30 years until he chose to share it in a speech at a conference for professional speakers in Asia. The process helped him to realise that he had locked his spirit, his beliefs and his courage away in that box at the same time.

Writing the speech and sharing the story freed Jerome up. He started to recognise that he had nothing to be ashamed about – in fact quite the opposite. He had saved three girls and then failed to accept credit for his courage.

Rather than acknowledging and owning what had really happened, Jerome accepted an alternative narrative and locked the trauma away. How will that have affected him over the last 30 years and how much would that simple action have impacted on his life going forward?

Why Trying to Look Good is Counterproductive

The masks we wear may vary in size — we hold back from sharing so many things, ranging from small challenges to large trauma with those around us. Each time we lock our challenges in a box, however, we prevent people from seeing who we truly are and move a step further away from achieving resolution and an ability to move forward unencumbered.

Each time we lock our challenges in a box, however, we prevent people from seeing who we truly are.

The irony of all of this is that, generally speaking, people respond positively when we express vulnerability. The response to Jerome's speech in Asia was overwhelming.

Of course, there are always exceptions to the rule and children can be particularly unforgiving (particularly in a large public school like Pegine's), but in the long term I believe that finding people we trust and opening up to them leads to deeper, more meaningful and longer lasting friendships, as well as an ability to be more authentic and at ease with ourselves.

When we are open and honest people feel a deeper connection with us as humans. They recognise that we are flawed — just as they are — and a sense of competition and one-upmanship goes out of the window.

When we are open and honest people feel a deeper connection with us as humans.

Not sharing because we want to look good can work against us as much if not more than in our favour. Yes, there are times when we need to present a positive face to the world. But don't do so at the expense of finding solutions or freeing your mind.

3.

BEING STRONG

Closely aligned to the need to look good is the desire to be strong and to be seen as strong.

In the conversations I had during my research for this book, the theme of 'having a thick skin' and needing to fend for yourself came up time and time again. I believe that the need for self-preservation is core to our conditioning as human beings. Bullied children are told to 'stand up for yourself'; people racked by uncertainty and doubt told to 'pull yourself together'.

That's all fine and it has its place. Resilience seems to now be one of the most popular topics for company conferences, personal development and training days. But resilience alone won't see you through dark times. In fact, accepting that you are perhaps not as strong as you'd like to be and admitting vulnerability will boost your resilience because it will allow you to let other people in to help and support you.

Accepting that you are not as strong as you'd like to be and admitting vulnerability will boost your resilience.

And it's a lot easier to get to where we need to be if other people can show us the way.

Dawnna Rising

Dawnna St Louis provides a classic example of someone who was conditioned to be strong. And if you meet Dawnna today you will be impressed by a very successful, independent and powerful woman. But, as is so often the case, the image Dawnna presents to the world doesn't tell the whole story.

Dawnna told me that she was over 40 years old before she could truly trust another person and easily let them help her. It was a skill that she had to learn through brutal lessons and it took two suicide attempts before she could really let someone in.

Born just after Martin Luther King was assassinated and raised in an American South still experiencing segregation in the early 1970s, Dawnna was the daughter of an African-American mother and part Jamaican, part Italian father. At the age of seven her family moved from California to Florida, from a very middle class, mixed-race area that she describes as a 'melting pot' to Miami's 'hood.

With dark curly hair and hazel eyes, Dawnna had more of a Latino appearance and, as a result, didn't fit into the predominantly African-American Miami neighbourhood where her family moved in with her grandmother. Dawnna was bullied because of her appearance – she just didn't look like the other kids.

The shift from suburban California to the poor, segregated Florida neighbourhood riven with racism was a real culture shock for the young girl. That shock deepened when her mother moved them out of their grandmother's home into a predominantly Cuban area. Not being Cuban and not speaking any Spanish, the bullying and racism got worse. Told to stand up for herself, she found herself in a fight every week.

"After a while you lose your innocence and vulnerability," Dawnna told me, "and the ability to be honest and true. Asking for help is a huge weakness. You'd better stand up for yourself. That was kind of my upbringing."

Like Pegine, Dawnna found that the more she fought, the more respect she would earn. Her vulnerable and positive emotions had to be tucked away and hidden from the world.

"I had this really tough, hard exterior. In a moment's notice I could turn a joke into an attack to ensure that everyone knew that just because I laughed at something it didn't mean I was weak. But on the inside I was soft and hurting. After I instigated a fight with someone I would cry in the shower or into a pillow at night. The next day it would start all over again."

In a moment's notice I could turn a joke into an attack to ensure that everyone knew that just because I laughed at something it didn't mean I was weak. But on the inside, I was soft and hurting.

Moving every three years or so meant that Dawnna didn't form the strong bonds that often emerge over time during childhood. The few times she felt that she trusted somebody enough to confide in them, those confidences would be shattered after the friendship broke up. So, she simply learned to keep her mouth shut.

Really a Blessing?

By the age of 17 Dawnna was pregnant and then things took a turn for the worse. Her daughter Tia died when she was just five months old. In her devastation she was told by an aunt that it was all for the best. "What were you going to do with the baby anyway?" her aunt asked her. "What happened was really a blessing, right?"

"In my family there was no such thing as talking back. If an adult said something, that was gospel." She had to be strong and move on.

But by the time she was 19 Dawnna knew she had to move away and change her life. Advice from another adult was the final straw.

"I had a guidance counsellor who had explained to me that, based on the trajectory of my life, I would be no more than a woman who had five kids: three would be in jail, one would be dead, and one would follow in my footsteps. Those footsteps would be that of an addict with a serious cocaine problem. I would use government assistance, my children, and my body to get to my fix. I would never make it out of North Orlando."

Dawnna had a rusty old car that she had purchased for $300. She got into her car and drove north with no destination in mind other than to prove her guidance counsellor wrong. But once she passed Disney World in Orlando, she just kept going.

"After 12 hours of driving I decided to sleep. Being a street-smart kid, I knew better than to stop at a rest stop or a truck stop. They were hunting grounds for girls travelling alone. So, I drove my car deep into this wooded area. In the morning I was ready to go but my car was not. I was stranded with no way to get help."

'I Am Never Going to Starve to Death if You Keep Feeding Me!'

With no money and no way to repair the car, Dawnna lived homeless in the woods for two years. She tried begging in the nearby town but her reluctance to turn to other people for support even made that difficult for her.

Eventually, not seeing a way out, Dawnna considered suicide. Fortunately, she didn't see it through. She decided that she would die naturally from hunger soon anyway. But she still had her pride; she didn't want to prove her critics right.

Half a mile from her car was a YMCA. She knew that the manager, Pop, would come out early every morning, playing his boom box loudly and cleaning the windows. Dawnna decided to do something that went completely against her instincts and ask for his help.

"I went there and I begged him to let me take a shower. I told him that I just wanted to be clean before I died in the next few days. I just wanted my body to be clean when they found it – for my mother. Tears streamed down my cheeks and I felt humiliated by them.

"Still wanting to protect myself, I showered without ever closing my eyes or taking off all of my clothes. When I exited the shower wearing wet clothes, Pop chuckled a bit as if reading my mind. In my embarrassment for misjudging his kindness and not having anything to give in return, I rushed towards the door with a fleeting 'thanks'.

"He responded, 'No problem. I will see you tomorrow.'

"His words stopped me in my tracks. I replied, 'What?' He said, 'Come back tomorrow. If you don't die today, you're going to need another shower'."

Dawnna went back the next day and carried on going each day, offering to clean the windows and gym equipment in return for her shower. She and Pops talked while she cleaned.

"Before I showered, Pop asked me to share his breakfast with him. I was so hungry but so sceptical of his kindness. My stomach growled at the smell of the eggs and bacon. He said, 'I can't eat it all and it'll just go in the garbage so you can have the rest'. Pops left the counter for a moment. By the time he came back the plate was completely empty and I had disappeared to the shower. I yelled, 'I am never going to starve to death if you keep feeding me!'

"It was the first time I was actually vulnerable, truly vulnerable with someone, and it scared the crap out of me. I constantly questioned what he wanted from me which made those moments of vulnerability fleeting."

It was the first time I was actually vulnerable, truly vulnerable with someone, and it scared the crap out of me.

What shocked Dawnna was that Pop never wanted anything in return. When she found a job, she saved up some money and took $70 back to the YMCA. It was a huge amount for her at the time but she wanted to pay Pop for the water she had used and the food she had eaten.

Pop simply refused to take it. And he wasn't the only one.

A police officer, Officer Smiley, found Dawnna's car in the woods. Dawnna naturally expected to be arrested but instead Officer Smiley came by every day with peanut butter and jelly sandwiches and ate lunch while sitting on the bonnet of her car. After a couple of weeks, he introduced her to a local businessman, FJ Pillack.

FJ didn't just give her a job but also paid for her to stay in a motel room across the street from the office until she could get back on her feet. Dawnna asked him to deduct the cost of the motel from her pay. Like Pop, FJ refused.

"There were people being kind to me for no reason and it made me feel very uneasy. When you have a tough exterior, you do not know how to handle people being nice to you for no reason. They must have ulterior motives. Growing up in the 'hood you never want to owe anyone anything.

"These three men were all extremely kind to me, yet they never asked me for anything. It scared the hell out of me."

Dawna flourished under FJ and by 26 she had started her own tech consultancy, which she sold when she was 39, taking early retirement.

Where the Light Shines Through

There's a pattern that appears throughout Dawnna's story. Driven by the lack of acceptance by any of the communities in which she lived as a child, being able to show others that she was strong and didn't need their help was a key factor in developing her tough exterior and trying to blend in. Breaking that pattern has been an important step in being vulnerable and accepting other people's help.

"Quite often we worry about what people will think about our actions, our looks and our lives. They are not. It is our ego that makes us believe that people have an opinion about what we do. It is our ignorance that drives us to let their opinion shape our lives.

It is our ego that makes us believe that people have an opinion about what we do. It is our ignorance that drives us to let their opinion shape our lives.

"The more authentically I showed up, the less I cared about what people thought about me. The more vulnerable I was, the more courageous people thought I was and the more people could connect with me – the real me. Then I heard this amazing quote: 'Let people see the cracks because that is where the light shines through'"[5].

I talked at the start of this chapter about how closely related 'looking good' and 'being strong' are and I believe that Dawnna's story illustrates this perfectly. She was conditioned by her upbringing to be tough and resilient – by the bullying and racism she experienced and by the demands of her family that she stand up for herself.

That toughness led to a belief that everyone is inward-looking and driven by selfish motives. People won't help you without expectation of something in return. Those beliefs made it almost impossible for Dawnna to ask for help and extremely difficult to accept help when it was offered.

How easy do you make it for the people around you to offer you their help and support? Are you asking for help quickly enough or are you driven by a need to be independent, strong and to prove your abilities – to yourself as much as to other people?

Even the leading sports stars in the world have coaches who can spot their weaknesses and scope for improvement. Top businessmen have mentors to guide them on their next steps. If other people know that you are struggling and where they can help, they are far better positioned to support you on your journey.

We need to reframe our view of vulnerability, moving from seeing it as a sign of weakness and admitting defeat to seeing it as a step on our path to victory.

Being strong isn't a reason not to ask for help. In fact, being open to help and support from all angles is a sign of real strength.

4.

You're Not Alone

When I speak about vulnerability at conferences, I have a simple exercise that demonstrates a very powerful point.

On every seat or place there are two coloured cards – one red and one green. At the appropriate point in the presentation I ask the audience three questions. The questions represent challenges that members of the audience might face, such as balancing the pressure of different tasks and projects effectively, being confident speaking up in meetings or having a clear view of where their career is heading over the coming years.

After each question I ask the audience members to hold up one of the cards if it is relevant to them. They hold up the red card if they are faced with that challenge at the moment or the green card if they have faced it in the past and overcome it. What happens is so clear and obvious but, at the same time, exceptionally impactful.

Everybody in that audience has challenges and the vast majority will have felt alone in facing them. They may feel that others wouldn't understand what they are going through or that they would look foolish if they shared. Yet all of a sudden they find themselves among people who know exactly what they have been going through. Every single time I have run this exercise, the audience has been a sea of red and green. Very few don't hold up either card.

Every day we battle with challenges we feel isolated by. We look at our friends, family, colleagues and others around us and envy how they seem to have it all together. We look up at speakers on the stage and read books by the people we most admire and wish we could have everything in place in the way they do.

But we're fooling ourselves.

A number of years ago I met a woman at a business event who really impressed me. A power dresser and plain talker, she told everyone else what they needed to know and what they needed to do – and spoke a lot of sense. She was confident and powerful. She owned the room.

I got to know her better over a few weeks and we got on so well that I eventually asked her out on a date. I told her how I perceived her when I first met her at that meeting and how I had got to know her better. "On the outside, you're very strong and impressive," I told her, "but underneath I believe you have a lot of doubts and fears."

At that point she melted. I meant what I said honestly but I have since learned that many people would react the same way. We walk around wearing a mask to impress people, scared of showing our flaws and fearful that our doubts would set us apart from the crowd. And when someone allows us to drop that mask, we feel a huge surge of relief.

Life would be so much easier if we all walked around with red and green cards, wearing our vulnerability on our sleeves. But it's not that simple. Without the visual aids, we need to remind ourselves constantly that we're not alone.

Life would be so much easier if we all walked around wearing our vulnerability on our sleeves. But it's not that simple. Without the visual aids, we need to remind ourselves constantly that we're not alone.

On a Pedestal

I mentioned above how we look at celebrities, speakers and authors and envy them their perfect lives. Many of the stories in the news recently should be starting to help people realise that life is not that simple. In fact, the morning I am typing this chapter, the news in the UK is focused on former England rugby international Danny Cipriani talking about struggling with suicidal thoughts shortly after his former girlfriend, TV presenter Caroline Flack, took her own life.

Over the entire journey of writing this book such stories have become more and more commonplace. But they are not new.

Leon Mackenzie has described it as his 'greatest day in football'. In the 66th minute of the English Premiership clash at Carrow Road, the Norwich City striker volleyed home from close to the penalty spot, his most memorable goal of a 15-year career. That winner, against a Manchester United side at the peak of their powers, with superstars like Wayne Rooney and Cristiano Ronaldo in their ranks, would have sent a lot of Norwich fans home happy that evening and the celebrations would have carried on well into the night. But despite his celebrations on the pitch, the aftermath of the game wasn't so enjoyable for Leon.

"When I was scoring goals against United and Chelsea, I was going through the worst time in my life and no one would know," Leon told me. "I was going through a horrible divorce, off the field situations, missing my children.

"The adrenaline rush was there in the moment but, when the game finished, I just went home, shut my door and sat there thinking. All I wanted to do was to see my kids but I couldn't."

Celebrities are human beings too, and beyond the glamour there's a lot going on under the surface. For Leon, his public face and his private persona were definitely two different worlds. And that had a very strong impact on his mental health.

"It brings out more emotions when you achieve something so big but yet feel so alone inside. If you are a fan paying to watch a person, you do not know what is going on in that person's life, regardless if they have just scored the 90th-minute winner.

"I got to a stage where I was a good pretender. I became a really good actor. I would come into the training ground bubbly. No one would ever know I was sad inside. A lot of that is pride as a man and also because you are in a position to be judged. No one really wants to be judged in a negative way."

Leon struggled with depression throughout his career but kept his struggles very private. Things reached a head when Leon was playing for Charlton Athletic towards the end of his career. Injury had become a real trigger and after leaving the training ground one afternoon, having pulled his hamstring, he finally opened up to his mother. He called her to tell her that he needed to retire. It was the first time that he had opened up to anyone and he then took some drastic action.

For a while Leon had been asking the doctor at Charlton for different medications for various ailments, and collecting them. After leaving training following his latest injury, he went back to the hotel where he had been living since moving clubs and swallowed his collection of pills.

"I wasn't living in my family home, I was away from my kids, I was away from everything. I was really alone. I was psychologically damaged. I knew I wasn't coping with my career ending. That is all it was really down to."

Fortunately, Leon immediately called his father who was just 20 minutes away and rushed him to hospital where he received treatment in time.

I am a Charlton fan and remember Leon's time with us very well. In the stands we didn't know the background, how Leon had battled with his demons and the impact injuries and fears of retirement were having on him. We didn't know about the lonely life in the hotel room, the separation from his family. All we saw was a player underperforming.

It is fortunate for Leon that social media wasn't in full swing at the time. After my conversation with Leon I look at the comments on Twitter after a poor Charlton performance and am horrified. Players are vilified after a defeat (and deified the following week after a win) and people ensure that the team's players are tagged in their posts so that they can reach them directly.

In such circumstances it's no wonder that we are hearing more and more about mental health breakdown among celebrities. If you are already full of doubt, the abuse from hundreds or thousands of strangers can only make things worse.

We're All the Same

On a more positive note, I think it is incredibly helpful to know that the people we admire the most have their own battles.

When people tell me that they could never do what I do and speak in public, the first thing I do is explain how I feel when I am presenting at a major conference. I tell them about the negative voice inside my head calling me a fraud just before I go on stage. I tell them how I panic in the belief that everything I planned to say will go out of my mind. I tell them how my body reacts to the fear in the build-up to my speech, how my heart beats faster, I sweat profusely and rush off to the toilet. When they tell me that they would never know any of that to look at me on stage, I tell them, "Exactly, and if I can do that then so can you."

In chapter 1 I shared how Hattie Webb had to learn how to deal with anxiety attacks after fainting on stage in Denmark. Some of the biggest support she received in the process came from two of the biggest stars she worked with, Leonard Cohen and American rock star Tom Petty.

Hattie told me, "In today's climate, people are beginning to open up about their anxiety or their feelings of inadequacy or imposter syndrome. It's coming from people that you never would have thought would feel this way – perhaps because of their level of success and what we perceive to be their perfect lives.

"I think it's really important to be vulnerable, particularly in creative industries, sharing and communicating. To know you're dealing with a human that expresses and cares makes a big difference.

"We were going on stage in Austin, Texas. Leonard was making coffee and as he was pouring his coffee I could see his hand shaking with nerves. He looked around to me with a smile and said, 'I've been doing this for 45 years and still…' I smiled back, knowing that we are all vulnerable.

"When we toured with Tom Petty and the Heartbreakers, one night in Vancouver Tom turned around to us on the way to the stage and said, 'I'm so nervous'. I felt more at ease with my nerves knowing Tom had them too.

"It's strangely reassuring when anyone else talks of their vulnerabilities. If you feel like you're in it with someone else, it feels less daunting."

It's strangely reassuring when anyone else talks of their vulnerabilities. If you feel like you're in it with someone else, it feels less daunting.

5.

HOW CAN WE TRUST
AND BE TRUSTED?

It was Mother's Day in Australia and Vanessa Hall's nine-year-old son had brought her a card he had made at school together with breakfast in bed. Vanessa opened the card and read her son's loving words: 'My mum is loving and caring', it read. 'She likes to buy lots of clothes, she always writes and reads. Sometimes she can keep promises but the best thing about my mum is that she is always there for me.'

"I thought that was really sweet," Vanessa told me, "but I was like, what do you mean 'sometimes'? Sometimes she keeps promises?

"He said, 'You just don't always keep your promises'. I asked, 'Like what? Like when? Give me an example'. 'Well, like a couple of weekends ago you said we would go to the movies on the weekend and then we didn't go.'

"I remembered what had happened. We had got busy and people popped in and things just got in the way. I said to him, 'But that wasn't a promise' and he said, 'But I thought it was.'

I said to him, 'But that wasn't a promise' and he said, 'But I thought it was.'

"I started to think about all the times I had done that with him and then I started to think about all the times we do that with everybody. I asked him, 'What happens when I do that? How does that make you feel?' He was sitting on the edge of my bed and he looked me straight in the eye and said, 'I don't know when I can trust you'."

Her son's shocking honesty really struck Vanessa and she was determined to truly understand what compels us to trust, what compels others to trust us, and how and why we damage the trust that is placed in us. Since then she has made it the major focus of her work, including writing an impressive book on the topic, *The Truth About Trust in Business* [6].

While it might be easy for some people to open up and share their innermost fears and challenges with all and sundry, for others it's tough to let a crack show in their armour to even their closest friends and family. We all have different approaches to trusting people around us, influenced by so many factors in our upbringing and life experiences.

I wanted to speak to Vanessa so that I could better understand how we learn to trust or distrust others and what we can do to find people in whom we are happy to confide. If we can't develop a trusted circle around us, then it's almost impossible for us to feel safe and secure opening up and being truly transparent and vulnerable.

If we can't develop a trusted circle around us, then it's almost impossible for us to feel safe and secure opening up and being truly transparent and vulnerable.

Vanessa told me that trust is something we can't generalise. "We trust based on the expectations and the needs that we each individually have. Our expectations come from our own experiences in the past.

"Studies in neuroscience and psychology highlight just how expectations are formed. Someone who has had bad experiences where they have been hurt will develop a series of negative expectations. Some will then generalise, it's the 'All men are bastards' theory."

Who Do We Trust?

Vanessa outlined several areas that influence why we trust each other, ranging from openness and transparency, through serving and humility to walking your talk and reliability. But, in her experience, people reach for just one quality.

"People might say, 'If you are honest then people will trust you' but that's not necessarily always true. There are plenty of honest people who others don't trust because there are other things going on, negative expectations or past experiences with similar people.

People might say, 'If you are honest then people will trust you' but that's not necessarily always true.

"Trust is a bit like beauty, it is in the eye of the beholder. I choose to trust you and it may or may not have anything to do with who you are and have everything to do with my own experience."

The Big Issue with Trust

One person who understands the role that past experience plays in people being willing to trust is Stephen Robertson. Stephen is the Chief Executive Officer of The Big Issue Foundation. The Foundation is the charitable arm of *The Big Issue*, the publication sold by homeless people in the UK that is designed to help them to get back on their feet and start their own small business.

The Foundation seeks to address the issues that made people homeless in the first place, or that they face once on the streets. Helping people whose experiences have led them to homelessness is not straightforward and those experiences do not necessarily make them naturally inclined to trust those who want to support them.

Stephen explained, "A feature of *The Big Issue* vendors' early experiences is running away and that trait is something that you can repeat. So, you run away from your relationship, you run away from your responsibilities with your job. That might not be physically, you might turn to drinking to numb something. Whatever that might be, the concept of absenting oneself is learned young and repeated.

"Asking for help can be quite a difficult thing if you've needed help in the past and, for whatever reason, it has not been there, has not been appropriate or has been withdrawn.

"One of the things that *The Big Issue* selling process enables or requires of you to make your business work is to begin to open up because you have to connect to people."

The Big Issue model is predicated on homeless people becoming magazine vendors and buying their stock before selling it on. It's designed to replace a reliance on handouts with self-sufficiency and independence. The need to engage with customers in order to drive more sales is also designed to build self-esteem. And that hopefully changes the relationship the vendors have with trusting others.

Stephen continued, "It's about dealing with the kind of everyday things that make sure you move forward and that your customers first and foremost are the people who are helping change you. If you can make a success of your business, you're getting that confidence so you become more conversational and you're actually quite proud you sold 50 magazines today.

"You can tell a lot about someone's wellbeing by how many magazines they sell; if they suddenly drop off then there must be an issue. You can map and understand what is going on, and if you understand that and you understand how to talk with people, then you will find that you have a greater chance of them opening up."

Brokering Trust in Partnerships

As a partnership broker, facilitating successful joint ventures between commercial and third sector organisations necessitates a deep understanding of trust and its ability to make or break a partnership. This is central to Catherine Russ's work and she explained to me just how important trust is to her work.

"In partnerships honesty and transparency is probably even more critical because you cannot hide from anybody. With social media and technology everything you do is going to be known, heard or talked about. If you want to be trusted, you need to make sure that what you are doing connects and has integrity with what you are presenting to your partnership. Often you will present an amazing front but your partners may be picking up something completely different that is being relayed by social media about you or your organisation.

"People often talk about how trust takes a long time to build up and can then very quickly dissolve. I have a different opinion of that: I think you can build trust quite quickly by being reliable, saying what you do and doing what you say. Revealing something humble about yourself is, I think, a fast track to building trust. You are not sharing this stuff to build yourself up, you are sharing just to show your authenticity and, to be honest, authenticity is short in this world."

Catherine has been party to a lot of instances where an unwillingness to be completely open with partners has led to diminishing trust between the parties, but as soon as that changes and people are finally able to talk about the elephant in the room, everyone breathes freely again.

Fail Fests

Catherine told me that she'd come across some organisations in the humanitarian sectors that hold 'Fail Fests'. Everyone is encouraged to come to a joint meeting where they discuss their projects with particular focus on where they have not worked out. They explore why certain initiatives didn't succeed and what they can learn from it in an environment focused on learning rather than blame.

It is hard to see this approach catching on easily in 'dog-eat-dog' commercial environments but wouldn't it be wonderful if it did? How might we truly innovate if we explore our mistakes and how might people be more willing to learn if we open up and share where things have gone wrong? For those that do this well it's not just talking about 'failure' in isolation that makes this work, it's the lessons learned that provide the value.

To get to this stage we need to build trusting environments. Safe spaces like these Fail Fests where people know they can share without fear of judgment or a negative impact on their career.

We need to build trusting environments. Safe spaces where people know they can share without fear of judgment or a negative impact on their career.

How Can We Be More Trusting?

You might recognise the importance of trusting others if you are going to let them help and support you but still find it hard to allow yourself to do so. If that's the case, Vanessa believes that there are two ways in which you can challenge your current mindset to allow yourself to become more trusting.

"The first part is being aware. I find a lot of people are very distrustful but aren't necessarily aware of that. I find that hard to comprehend; it's impossible to not trust, we trust every day.

"If people are going into a job or a relationship and they are expecting that there is going to be trouble or that they will be micromanaged or that they are going to be betrayed in some way, they will behave consistently with that. We all behave consistently with our expectations, positive or negative, which often creates a self-fulfilling prophecy.

"We then go in guarded; we protect ourselves. We don't share information and we can often be seen as being obstructionist or not cooperative. This is where we often think it's about everyone else, 'I can't trust other people', but it's more about understanding yourself and how you are showing up."

Fifteen years on, Vanessa's relationship with her son is extremely close. Many of their friends who have heard her story ask him what his mum is like at keeping promises these days. He jokes that she is much more careful and doesn't make as many!

One single observation by a nine-year-old completely changed Vanessa's awareness of the impact of our words on others and started her on a journey to change our understanding of the importance of trust and its role in society.

6.

How Do Self-Compassion and Gratitude Impact on our Ability to Ask for Help?

Jerome's story, shared in chapter 2, highlighted a major stumbling block on the road to being vulnerable and allowing others to help us. Jerome put his own needs and personal respect to one side, and accepted the narrative that he should be ashamed of the assault on him.

Learning to be kind to yourself, to give yourself a break and showing gratitude to others can make it easier for you to allow others to support you. And asking for that support is likely to have a positive impact on your career.

Learning to be kind to yourself, to give yourself a break and showing gratitude to others can make it easier for you to allow others to support you.

Those are the findings of a pilot study that a team of researchers in Chicago ran in tandem with the writing of this book. Forty-six participants from a range of backgrounds in seven countries participated in the research, which involved them going through a 12-week training programme, including ten modules on networking. Participants were also provided with a variety of exercises designed to help increase both gratitude and self-compassion.

Research lead John Jameson told me, "What has come back from the pilot study was that there was a correlation between people who are self-compassionate and a willingness to ask for help. The assumption of this book is that asking for support helps us to overcome adversity. Having the right support in your network and in relationships helps you to be successful. We were determining whether or not gratitude and self-compassion are related to asking for help and the study establishes that link.

"Furthermore, what we found is that people who are more willing to ask for help have achieved higher levels in their career. People who were more willing to ask for help were at a director or executive level versus entry level."

As Job Level Increases, So Does Self-Compassion

The finding that participants at director/VP/executive level are more self-compassionate than participants at the entry and mid-level jobs suggests that employees at higher levels may be less critical of themselves and accept their imperfections.

John remarked that this is an unsurprising finding and may have as much to do with experience in general as with seniority. "With maturity many learn to accept their imperfections and be a bit gentler on themselves. Furthermore, we found that people who are more self-compassionate are also more likely to demonstrate gratitude. So, if I am grateful for the knowledge, skills, experiences and relationships that I have, there is a higher likelihood that I will be more self-compassionate."

John believes that there may be a generational aspect to asking for help. "That's a trend that we have seen over and over for years. We can point the finger at social media, where the airbrushed version of everyone's lives perpetuates the issue. Letting go of comparison is something that they need to do.

"One participant in his early 20s ended up making a job transition because he was hired by a financial services company and left because he wasn't adequately trained on how to do his job. Rather than asking for help and looking unqualified, he changed organisation.

"Letting go of perfectionism is a challenge for many and self-compassion, including accepting your faults, is an important element of being able to do that. Ceding control to others or letting them in is never easy, particularly for a perfectionist."

Letting go of perfectionism is a challenge for many and self-compassion, including accepting your faults, is an important element of being able to do that.

One study participant reported to researchers, "Realising and being OK with the fact that I cannot do everything personally all the time makes asking for assistance easier, especially when I am turning a project over to someone else. Giving up control is hard! I have been accustomed to taking the lead, so stepping aside so someone else can help or be in the spotlight affects all aspects of life."

We also found that seniority in job title gives the individual greater confidence in their position and in their right to request support.

John continued, "A lot of participants who didn't want to ask for help were held back by their assumptions that other people wouldn't want to help them, that they would inconvenience the other person, or be rejected. Such fears are less likely to prey on the mind of people in more senior roles. On the other hand, if people are used to giving help to others, they will be aware of the positive feeling that can be induced and might expect that others would get the same pleasure from helping them.

"Many don't want to be perceived as weak or unqualified by asking for help. If I don't ask for help, then I don't get rejected. This is a common self-defence mechanism. For whatever reason we take rejection personally, which leads to negative emotions that in turn can affect self-esteem. How many people have been shot down asking someone for a date and then they never ask again? It requires a certain level of resilience.

"On the other side of the assumption is the release of dopamine in the brain when something feels good, like helping. So, if it feels good for me to help another, then I am more likely to ask for help to give others that opportunity."

Vulnerability as a Self-Development Tool

One of the participants in the survey said, "When I was young I thought asking for help was a weakness, but as I matured I realised it was not only necessary but a strength." The study demonstrated that many of the participants who were already successful and happy to ask for help recognised that they didn't know everything and that the answers they sought often lay in their network.

John saw this come through strongly. "Something else that emerged was evidence of the relationship between learning and asking for help. On a very basic level, learning is a primary reason we ask for help. It's not always just for a solution; we ask because we want to learn.

On a very basic level, learning is a primary reason we ask for help. It's not always just for a solution; we ask because we want to learn.

"One participant also drew a parallel between asking for help and leadership. Conventional theories suggest that the leader is wise and all knowing. But, over time, leadership has become more about engaging the diverse opinions of employees, asking for help and appealing to their individual expertise."

Another participant showed how their desire for improvement and learning had overtaken the fear of looking bad as they had matured. They reported, "Falling short can result in a softer landing. What that means to me is that every learning experience from falling will make me stronger and that results in the service I provide being more beneficial to the recipients.

"Risk reduction was historically a big deal for me. Now, exposure of faults is seen as a pre-emptive measure and an opportunity to improve. My ego is still maturing but I believe I am finally beyond adolescence."

The Importance of Trust

Many people will assume that trust is the foundation of any willingness to open up and ask for help but attitudes to trust varied among the participants.

"I would say that individuals don't necessarily need to trust the person who they are asking but rather be able to qualify the information that they are receiving as good and reliable," said John.

He also explained how trust was mentioned as a rapport-building mechanism. "Someone can proactively build trust with employees by asking for help; even just asking for help with something small is a good way to assess trust."

In my experience, this can work both ways and I would argue that people would be more inclined to trust and be open to a deeper relationship with people who ask them for their help and advice. We like to be asked for our opinion and have our experience and abilities valued. Therefore, asking for help in the way outlined by John would be likely to lead to more positive engagement, whether at work or personally.

Be Grateful

One of the central pillars of the pilot study was the importance of gratitude. The study showed evidence that supports the claim that participants who expressed gratitude were more skilled in developing relationships. The study also established a link between gratitude and a belief that asking for help has positively impacted on their career.

One participant reported, "Gratitude for all past experiences, knowledge and relationships leads to increased confidence, a sense of identity and value to others."

The research provided evidence that a relationship exists between showing gratitude and being able to ask for and receive support. Demonstrating that you appreciate and value others may give them a sense of confidence and a sense of value. In turn, they may be more inclined to help you in the future. You are helping them by asking for help.

Demonstrating that you appreciate and value others may give them a sense of confidence and a sense of value. In turn, they may be more inclined to help you in the future.

One participant reported, "Humility helps. When you are grateful you have a better chance of having a relationship and it's easier to reach out to those with whom you have a relationship." While another stressed, "Being grateful is humbling to me. Being humble allows me to be more vulnerable."

Both self-compassion and gratitude are clear themes that show up time and again in the stories shared in this book. It's clear that valuing yourself and showing your appreciation for the love and support of the people who surround you open the doors to allowing your network to be there for you. And it's that support that has helped many of the people interviewed for this book turn their lives around.

The research John and his team have started to explore reinforces the importance of these qualities. A report on the pilot study to date is available at: www.andylopata.com/justaskstudy

SECTION TWO
SETTING YOUR
STRATEGY

7.

WHAT'S YOUR PURPOSE?

I have been told time and again over the last few years that this is a book that people are ready to read. The importance of being vulnerable and of allowing other people to support us has gained traction in the last decade. But a generic message encouraging people to 'be vulnerable' isn't enough. We need to know when and where to be vulnerable, who with, how and, most importantly, why.

The aim of this book is not to create an army of readers who tell everybody everything that is going on in their lives. Who, when asked 'How are you?' or 'How's work?' list every challenge and every tragedy in every conversation. Whose every social media update is a cry for help or a tale of woe.

We need to be much more thoughtful about the way we open up and ask for help than that. Failure to do so will damage relationships and reputation as well as see support dry up as we get seen as the 'boy who cried wolf'.

I'll come on to some of the other questions later in this section but for now I want to focus on the 'why?'.

The Power of Purpose

There are many possible reasons why we might need other people's support. For both professional and personal reasons and for businesses as well as individuals, the ability to be open and vulnerable can be a powerful asset. Meanwhile, the challenges we share can range from simple questions to life-changing decisions.

One thing that has become clear to me, however, is that having a clear purpose makes it much easier to ask for help. If you understand why you need support and what benefits you'll gain from the input of others, you will be far more focused on asking. It becomes even more natural when that objective impacts people other than you.

If you understand why you need support and what benefits you'll gain from the input of others, you will be far more focused on asking.

Over the last few years Andy Agathangelou has invested his time and energy in trying to achieve a drastic reform of the financial services industry, learning from the lessons of the financial crash and associated scandals to drive truth and trust across the sector.

That's no small challenge, particularly in an industry with many powerful vested interests who might not necessarily appreciate Andy's efforts. Despite that, his 'Transparency Task Force' has had an impact globally and many leading influencers across financial services have become actively involved.

Trying to influence a major change in an extremely powerful industry meant that Andy first had to focus on changing his approach and outlook. His tendency to get his head down and plough towards a goal on his own, combined with a loathing for asking for help, left him in financial difficulties.

At the beginning, driven by doing the right thing, he put aside his day-to-day work to focus on the Transparency Task Force, while valiantly battling to do everything on his own. When he was on the verge of selling his car to find funds, Andy realised that he had a choice. He could go back to his day job and let his dream die or he could learn to ask for support.

"Frankly, I could not do it on my own," Andy explained. "Three individuals kindly helped me: they literally coached me on how to ask for help; they helped me to reframe what asking for help meant. They realised that my alpha male ego would not cope with asking for help for me personally, so they got me to think about not asking for help for me but asking for help for the cause.

They realised that my alpha male ego would not cope with asking for help for me personally, so they got me to think about asking for help for the cause.

"I can do that. I don't feel ashamed to ask for help for the cause because I totally believe in what we are trying to do and the reasons we are trying to do it. There is a slightly different mindset between asking for help for yourself and asking for help for something you believe in. That was the major emotional breakthrough. "Having learned to ask for help, I got help."

Creating Clarity

Andy's experience is not uncommon. I have spoken to many people who admit to struggling to ask for help for themselves but find it so much easier when they are asking for others, whether it be for other people or for a cause.

If this is you, focus your attention on what you are trying to achieve and how success impacts not just you but other people. Even if you feel that your need is selfish, there is a good chance that others will benefit from your success, whether it be friends and family, colleagues or others.

Take a moment to recognise where you are stuck, or simply not achieving your full potential at the moment. Where do you need help in your professional life? Where do you need help in your personal life? Is there a cause, a charity or a movement that you feel passionately about and you would like to support? Where do you need help to make a real impact?

In each case, how would your success or failure affect you personally? And how would it affect the people around you, whether directly invested in that scenario or simply as a result of the impact you make? Picture how other people would benefit if you were able to maximise your impact on that project, whether it's performing to your fullest ability, getting your dream job, raising substantial funds for charity or making your marriage a massive success.

If you can achieve clarity around how others are impacted by your success, then, like Andy, you are no longer asking for help just for yourself. If you are clear about your purpose and driven by what achieving that purpose will mean to the people around you, then asking for help suddenly becomes a whole lot easier.

If you are clear about your purpose and driven by what achieving that purpose will mean to the people around you, then asking for help suddenly becomes a whole lot easier.

Getting the support that you need frees you up to do the best you can to make a positive impact on other people's lives. That seems like a cause worth being vulnerable for.

8.

LET OTHER PEOPLE IN

How do you feel when you help someone you like or love? Particularly when you know that your support has had a positive impact?

Most of us feel satisfied when we get the opportunity to help other people. Particularly when they make it easy for us to do so. I believe that it's in our nature to want to support others and to take pleasure from giving that support. It even feeds our ego, making us feel useful and important.

I always find it bizarre that we stop ourselves from asking other people for their help and support, partly because we don't want to be a burden to them. Yet we derive so much pleasure from helping others. Surely, by not asking for help we are depriving other people of that pleasure!

I always find it bizarre that we stop ourselves from asking other people for their help and support, partly because we don't want to be a burden to them. Yet we derive so much pleasure from helping others.

Murderball

Two of the people I interviewed for this book both had to come to terms with relying on other people for support after experiencing life-changing disability.

Andy Barrow heard a loud crack while he was in a scrum during the last game of his first year of senior rugby. "I felt a searing pain go through my neck," Andy recalls, "my ears popped louder and deeper than ever before or since and I heard a scream. That scream was me."

He was airlifted to a local hospital where they told him he had broken his neck and severely damaged his spinal cord.

"Breaking my neck wasn't the worst day of my life, that came about five days later. I had a conversation with a nurse that changed my life forever. Wayne came on to my ward, pulled the curtains back and said, 'I need to tell you something. I've heard you've been talking about walking out of here, talking about the possibility of making a full recovery. There is no chance of you making a full recovery. There is not even a chance of you making a partial recovery. You are not going to walk again'."

Andy spent five months in hospital facing the long road to rehabilitation. He was paralysed from the chest down, with approximately 20% of the body function of an able-bodied person.

You might think that suffering an injury of that magnitude would affect an active, sports-obsessed youth like Andy even more than it would others but Andy's passion for sport came to his rescue.

"Being physically fit was vital so that I could continue my life in the most independent fashion possible. That word, *independence*, was a massive motivator. My survival wasn't in doubt but my independence was."

Rehabilitation instructors came in to introduce the patients to a range of disabled sports. Unsurprisingly, given his background, Andy immediately fell in love with wheelchair rugby (known as quad rugby in the US).

"Wheelchair rugby was invented by a bunch of guys with my disability because they were not able enough to play wheelchair basketball. So, they took wheelchair basketball and tweaked it to be more friendly to their functionality. I know the people who invented this and they probably sat there and looked at that and thought 'this is not quite scratching the itch; we are going to smash into each other and we'll call it murderball'."

Andy's competitive instincts kicked in and soon murderball, or wheelchair rugby as it became better (and more respectfully) known, became much more than therapy. Andy captained his national team, representing Great Britain in three Paralympic Games, three World Championships and five European Championships – three times winning gold medals. At his peak Andy was ranked in the top five players in the world in his classification.

Moving Mountains

Like Andy, David Lim also had to come to terms with a sudden shift from being an able-bodied, high-achieving athlete to living with a disability.

David made his name leading the first Singapore expedition to the peak of Mount Everest. Coming from a country more focused on economic achievement than sporting glory, David compares his expedition as a bit of an oxymoron, something like the Jamaican Olympic bobsled team!

Leading his team to the peak was a bittersweet achievement. Just one week after their triumphant return to Singapore, and completely unrelated to the expedition, he was struck down by the rare nerve disorder Guillain-Barré syndrome. He was paralysed from the eyes down and spent the next 43 days on a ventilator.

As the nerves recovered David had to teach himself the basics again, how to write and how to feed himself. Twenty years later David still has disabilities in his lower legs, left hand and the left side of his face. David told me how he picked up his passion for mountaineering very quickly after leaving hospital.

"In January 2000, about a year after I was discharged, I went to climb the highest mountain in North and South America, Aconcagua. It was a totally different kind of expedition compared to the usual large-scale Himalayan expeditions, meaning no professional guides, no Sherpas, no fixed ropes – none of the trappings you usually have."

David learned fairly quickly that his abilities had been affected by the nerve disorder and he would have to adapt. "I had one partner only, Wilfred, and we were making the approach to base camp at Aconcagua. During the approach, which is a three-day march, there are a number of river crossings, which you have to do early while the water levels are still around ankle height.

"Imagine crossing a river in bare feet and sometimes the water is knee high. Worst of all, there are even sections where we had to jump across rocks to get to the other side. With my very compromised balance and disabilities it was enormously difficult for me and each crossing took about 45 minutes.

"The first two days everything was hunky-dory, we were coping with everything really well. It was only the last day going up to base camp that we had these river crossings to make. At the first one you think 'I can do it, I just need to balance a bit more slowly'. It was excruciating; time was wasted looking for easier ways to get across.

"Eventually we realised, contrary to various accounts, it wasn't just three river crossings, it looked like there were going to be at least ten to make. I think the penny dropped after lunch. We had about six hours of daylight and we were nowhere close to base camp. Wilfred told me, 'If we don't change the way we are working together, it's going to be nightfall before we get there.'

"Throughout this journey I had refused to ask for help. Wilfred was an able-bodied person, and he was a strong technical climber but he didn't have as much experience as I did in terms of high-altitude mountaineering experience. I refused to accept that I had a different body altogether."

Eventually David accepted that he needed help. They changed their approach so that Wilfred would take his pack across, come back to pick up David's and then meet David halfway across. Each crossing now took only five minutes.

"I realised that, in any situation that came up, by asking for help when I needed it we were working so much better as a team. That was a huge thing that made me realise that sometimes when people have been successful in their past, irrespective of their present situation, that success might actually be a handicap because they refuse to ask for help.

When people have been successful in their past, irrespective of their present situation, that success might actually be a handicap because they refuse to ask for help.

"What gets in the way, I think, is ego, and the belief that past performance equals present performance. What re-enforced it was Wilfred saying, 'You're not the same guy that you used to be'."

Shades of Grey

Both Andy and David found that they initially didn't face a choice over whether or not to rely on other people's help. Circumstances had made them completely reliant on the support of others. In time and with some readjustment, that made it much easier for them to accept help and support.

"One of the advantages for me was that it was so black and white," Andy told me. "With spinal cord injuries you need help with some very personal things in the beginning. But then a lot of grey areas came about, so still to this day there will be people with the same severity of disability who will allow other people to dress them and help with day-to-day bathroom activities for them whereas I didn't. I battled what I could but I was fairly quick to understand which battles to pick. I still will, I'll still try to do as much as I can for myself."

Both Andy and David showed a strong independent spirit but David found it more of a struggle to accept the things that he couldn't do. He said, "When the situation is extremely obvious there is no choice. It's only in grey areas, where you are still capable of doing something but you're really doing it very slowly, very badly, then what is preventing you from asking for help is just your ego.

"I was angry but the anger or the resentment was rarely directed towards those people trying to help me; it was very much directed towards the situation.

"Eventually I had to realise that if you don't ask for help, you don't get it."

Reaching Acceptance

David has learned now to adapt to his disability, accepting help where necessary but still pushing himself. He still climbs actively but adapts his approach accordingly.

"The more that you have help, the less the satisfaction of the achievement being *your* achievement."

Andy has also learned to accept help, although it's an area he struggles with more than others. It may be a work in progress but Andy admits that he has come a long way from the early days and recognises the importance and power of accepting help.

"One of the most empowering things you can do is ask for and provide help. It's something we should all be doing more often, whether in a personal or professional context."

One time where this plays out in a really lovely safe way is when I go to Glastonbury Festival and I have to ask. Let's just say I need help 5% of the time in the everyday world; at Glastonbury I need help at least 50% of the time because I'm travelling around a field. That experience, albeit a very sanitised, contrived experience, is wonderful.

"I remember the first year my wife and I went, I was still working on 'outside of Glastonbury' parameters. That led to the two of us shouting at each other in a field one night. That made me realise that I was assuming that help would come from just one person. As soon as that switch flipped, I was asking everyone for help, or not asking but accepting help from everyone. People would ask, 'Can we help you?' I would say, 'Yes, push me as far as you want; as soon as you don't want to go where I want to go, walk off and we will part our ways'. We met all of these amazing people."

It's only with asking for help that you become more experienced at asking for help.

It's only with asking for help that you become more experienced at asking for help.

Willing to Accept Help Every Day

The examples of Andy and David may seem extreme. If you're not incapacitated, you don't need help to the same degree that they do. But despite the clear and compelling cases for assistance in both of their lives, they both resisted.

And that's something many of us are conditioned to do all the time. We are conditioned to prove that we are capable of doing things ourselves. This goes to the root of the problem with a lack of vulnerability and shows up in all areas of our lives. The support that we need is all around us and our lives become easier and healthier when we turn and embrace that support. But something stops us from doing so.

Being willing to let people in and allow them to help doesn't need to detract from our independence or abilities. Asking people to help is not the same as allowing others to do things for you. It's neither delegation nor abdication, it's collaboration.

Asking people to help is not the same as allowing others to do things for you. It's neither delegation nor abdication, it's collaboration.

That is something that we can learn from, that makes us stronger and which helps us to deliver more positive results. But we need to open the door first.

9.

ANSWERING THE KEY QUESTIONS

I keep six honest serving-men

(They taught me all I knew);

Their names are What and Why and When

And How and Where and Who.

Rudyard Kipling, *The Elephant's Child*

R ead any advice on strategy and there is a fair chance that, at some point, you will come across Kipling's famous poem. I'm not claiming any points for originality in quoting it here! I am a great believer, however, that clichés become so for a reason, because they are relevant and serve a purpose.

Once you have accepted that it is beneficial to break the mould of being seen to be independent, strong and all-knowing, it is important to ask yourself those famous questions from Kipling's poem.

- *What do you need to talk about?*

- *Why are you sharing?*

- *When is the right time to share?*

- *How much should you share?*

- *Where do you share?*

- *With whom do you share?*

What Do You Need to Talk About?

For many of us there is a lot going on in our lives at any one time. In my experience, however 'together' somebody appears on the surface, I have rarely met someone who doesn't have something going on. A milestone they are trying to achieve or a challenge they are struggling to overcome in either their personal or professional lives. If not both.

We can feel overwhelmed at times with the decisions we need to make and the issues we have to deal with. And we can't pass on that overwhelm to others by burdening them with all of our problems when they ask how we are.

It may be that once we have accepted the power of being vulnerable, we share different parts of our lives with different people. Whether we do that or we're simply selective in the challenges we choose to unload, those issues need to be prioritised. Which challenges are we comfortable and capable of dealing with on our own? Where will we most benefit from the expertise, experience or perspective of those we trust?

It may be that once we have accepted the power of being vulnerable, we share different parts of our lives with different people.

Creating focus on which areas of our lives we choose to seek support with feeds the rest of the questions we need to answer. If we know what we want to share, then we can start asking ourselves why that is so important to us and what we want to achieve by being vulnerable.

Why Are You Sharing?

Sometimes we just need to vent. In other cases we are looking for advice and, ideally, solutions. Either is fine, we just need to have some clarity about what results we are looking for from our conversations.

If it's important for us to know the 'why', it's even more important for the people to whom we open up. Our supporters need to know whether or not we are open to their advice, if we want them to take some action to help us or whether we just need someone there to listen.

Once you know what you need to talk about, ask yourself exactly the type of support you need and how that will impact the challenge you face. Then, when seeking to share with others, start by sharing why you need the conversation and how you think they can help.

When is the Right Time to Share?

When Ivan Misner was diagnosed with prostate cancer, working out how to fight his illness was just one challenge he faced.

Ivan was the figurehead and CEO of the world's largest face-to-face business networking organisation, Business Network International (BNI). As much as he might have liked to focus on his medical challenges with just the support of family and close friends, he didn't have that option. Particularly as he had chosen to fight the cancer naturally, by drastically changing his diet.

Ivan told me how he planned to share the news with his wider network and different stakeholders in his business. "People are going to find out, they are going to ask, 'Why are you eating so crazy? Why are you losing weight?' I'm going to doctor's appointments all the time, so I figured just talk about the elephant in the room, calm everyone down and tell them that you have a plan.

"I made a list of eight different levels of people. Number one was extended family; my wife and kids were technically number one but they found out immediately. Number two, close family friends. Number three were key management people in the company, the top managers in BNI.

"Number four were the employees at headquarters. I literally called a staff meeting and said, 'Hey, this is what's going on, I just wanted you to know, what questions do you have for me? That was really important; if you don't let them ask their questions, they are going to be asking each other and they are going to be making stuff up.

"Franchisees worldwide were number five. The sixth one was global employees and independent contractors. Number seven was an email that directors could share with members and number eight was a public posting on my blog."

Ivan was inspired by self-development guru Brian Tracy, who had suffered from throat cancer a couple of years before and who had been very open on his blog about his journey. Ivan resolved to share 'the good, the bad and the ugly', making sure that people would know at all times how he was progressing. He posted every three or four months for the first year and then once a year after that.

"It calmed everyone down. This may not work for everyone but I liked it because everyone knew I had a plan. I kept saying to them, 'If it doesn't work, I will go and get surgery, I promise.'

"You can't control the message but you can manage it. I was constantly managing the message, to the point of writing a book sharing the full story and the recipes that I used to completely change my diet"[7].

Timing is a key factor in ensuring that you benefit the most from sharing with the people around you. Leave something too long and you may find that you've missed the moment when other people's help would have been most effective or their suggestions would have worked. You also face the risk, as Ivan observed, that people notice for themselves that something is wrong and you start to lose control of the message.

Timing is a key factor in ensuring that you benefit the most from sharing with the people around you.

If you ask too early, you may feel that people will see you as someone who is not able to find solutions for themselves, who panics or who overshares. Every situation is different. Ivan calculated when he should share his news with each interested party to remain in control of the conversation. Think about the best time to share and whether different people need to be involved at different times.

How Much Should You Share?

After three rounds of IVF and a miscarriage, the still-birth of their twins was devastating for Kelly and her partner Lee. Coping with the trauma was bad enough but then another predicament raised its head: Kelly still had a visible bump so, to all appearances, she was still pregnant.

The thought of telling people individually was terrifying, let alone dealing time and again with the same questions. Kelly had been writing a blog about her IVF journey from the start of her second round and she and Lee decided to share their sad news there.

"I had just found it difficult to keep everything a secret," Kelly explained. "It was so hard, running a business and trying to attend all of my IVF appointments around it. Keeping this massive secret all the time and not being able to explain to people why all of a sudden you can't commit to meetings or plan in advance. It's just not me and I hated every minute of it, it felt deceitful.

"The blog had always been about helping other people, raising awareness. If you haven't been through it, it's completely overwhelming. That was one of the reasons we decided to share the news on the blog, because we had shared everything. If you're going to blog about a journey, you have to commit to the highs and lows and we were always adamant that we would."

One person who was most uncomfortable about Kelly's sharing was her business partner, Paul. Kelly had called me one evening earlier in her IVF journey. The blog had caught the attention of their local BBC radio station and one of the presenters, Chris Mann, had invited her on to his show to discuss her experiences. When Kelly called me, she was upset and confused. The interview was scheduled for the following day but Paul had told her that he didn't think she should go ahead.

"I was challenged, by my business partner, as to how that was going to come across for me. It really threw me; I didn't want to pull out but I now felt really uncomfortable."

Paul's reservations did not come from any mean-spirited attempt to protect the business or from a lack of understanding. In fact, Paul and his wife Amber fully understood what Kelly and Lee were going through. When Amber was 22 weeks through her first pregnancy, a routine scan uncovered something badly wrong with the baby and they lost it.

"It massively turned our world upside down," Paul told me. "Of course, everyone knew. Everyone knew that we were going to have this baby. I would find myself randomly bursting into tears just driving along. I still feel for Kel when she is bombarded with baby stuff because I always remember that. Everywhere you turned it would be about babies, about parenting.

"Amber didn't want to go out at all. It took a long time for her to want to see friends, she just hid herself away. For me I just wanted to get her through it and I think for me that got me through it as well, I felt like I should be the strong one.

"Other people tell you that they've had the same experience. Suddenly, you realise that you're not the only couple who have been through this; in fact, there are lots and lots of people but no one really speaks about it."

Suddenly, you realise that you're not the only couple who have been through this; in fact, there are lots and lots of people but no one really speaks about it.

Paul's concerns for Kelly at the time of the BBC radio interview were more focused on what would happen if things went well, if people who were still struggling with IVF would resent her and Lee getting good news. He was also concerned about how she would cope with sharing this news while emotionally vulnerable.

"For me it just would've seemed better to have kept it to yourself and go through the journey on your own rather than sharing it with everyone."

In my conversation with Paul I wanted to find out why he was so concerned about a possible backlash against Kelly. He admitted to being a very private person who finds the thought of being judged and being pitied, particularly by strangers, uncomfortable. Sharing one-to-one is not really a problem for him but opening up to a group is something very different.

In the end Kelly went ahead. During our phone call before the interview I asked her whether, a year before, somebody going on the show and talking about similar experiences would have helped her. Kelly replied, "It absolutely would." And then she told me, "I knew it was the right thing to do. And it was hard. But I did do it, and I'm really glad that I did."

I was fascinated by the conflict between the two different approaches: sharing everything openly and publicly on the one hand and keeping your counsel very much to yourself on the other.

Speaking with both Kelly and Paul it was clear to see that there is no right or wrong way to do things. In the next chapter we will explore the conflict between 'oversharing' and maintaining personal privacy on social media; the same conflict exists in our interpersonal 'real world' relationships too. People have different approaches to sharing.

My advice is to find the approach that suits you, while being aware that not everyone will be comfortable with it or feel that you are doing the right thing. If you are reading this book under duress and hate the thought of sharing even one intimate thought, then Kelly's approach will horrify you.

Find the approach that suits you, while being aware that not everyone will necessarily be comfortable with it.

But if you talk openly to everyone around you about what's happening in your life, you may struggle to understand how Paul could keep things to himself. And that's fine. We are different. Ultimately you need to be comfortable with how much you share. If you carefully consider where and with whom you share, you should be able to find a way that works for all parties.

Where Do You Share?

Social media's rise has given us a new supercharged opportunity to share more information, more frequently and to a much wider audience.

While social media has its place, though, I would still argue that face-to-face conversations will always be more personal and provide a greater opportunity to explore further.

Formal mastermind groups or mentoring relationships provide a perfectly structured opportunity to seek support in a trusted environment. In fact, it's expected of you if the ground rules are set as they should be. We'll explore these further in section 3.

If you struggle to find 'the right time' to ask someone for help, we have the opportunity several times each day and consistently ignore it. When greeting each other, people will often ask 'How are you?'. Sometimes it's OK to be honest when you reply.

When greeting each other, people will often ask 'How are you?'. Sometimes it's OK to be honest when you reply.

Most people ask 'How are you?' or its close companion 'How's work/business?' merely as a courtesy. It's our way of warmly opening a conversation. And the perennial 'I'm fine thanks, how are you?' is a perfectly appropriate and acceptable way to respond. You may, however, choose to be more honest.

Around the time I realised that I needed to be more vulnerable when my business was struggling, I bumped into a good friend of mine, a fellow speaker, at a private members' club in London. He asked me 'How's business?'... and I told him. I explained that the business was struggling and it had been a tough few months.

"I'm really sorry mate," he replied. Then he asked, "How can I help?"

I received two referrals from him in the next three weeks. He had never referred me before because, as he explained to me, he had never thought I needed the help.

If you greet someone you like and trust, who you would feel comfortable opening up to, then be honest when they ask how you are. Simply tell them that things are tough or you've had struggles without going into detail. Let them move the conversation on and accept the implicit invitation to explore further if they want to.

If you greet someone you like and trust, who you would feel comfortable opening up to, then be honest when they ask how you are. Let them move the conversation on and accept the implicit invitation to explore further if they want to.

There are two types of people who ask 'How are you?'. Those who are interested in the answer and those who are not. If they are not genuinely interested, they will say, 'I'm really sorry to hear that' and then move the conversation on to more comfortable ground. But if they are interested, as my friend was, they will seek to support you of their own accord.

Of course, you don't need to wait for people to ask how you are before you seek help. If you have taken the other steps in this chapter and know what type of help you want, it becomes a much simpler step to just pick up the phone and ask.

With Whom Do You Share?

When identifying the right people to share with, there are a number of key factors to consider.

Number one would be *trust*. Ideally, you want to trust the people you open up to not to judge you for it, to respect what you share in confidence, to understand the context and situation and, if appropriate, to give you the right advice.

Allied to that is that they are *qualified* to support you. This is particularly important if you are looking for their input and ideas. So, you might not share professional challenges with a friend or family member who doesn't understand the intricacies of what you are going through.

When I spoke with Andy Barrow, who we met in the last chapter, he told me of the difference it made to him discovering the wheelchair rugby community when he left hospital. Andy told me, "It's absolutely vital that when you are faced with extreme adversity you can turn to a group of people who have been in that position. It is massively important to have people who get you."

It is massively important to have people who get you.

Having said that, I think it can be dangerous just to turn to people in a similar position to you for support. By keeping the conversations within a close pool of people who share experiences and perspective, the flow of new ideas can be restricted. I strongly encourage you to mix who you share with, having a *diverse network* of people you can engage with so that you go outside the obvious group to people who might have a completely different perspective.

In his excellent 2019 book *Rebel Ideas*, Matthew Syed explained: 'Solutions to complex problems typically rely on multiple layers of insight and therefore require multiple points of view.' He goes on to quote American academic Philip Tetlock: 'The more diverse the perspectives, the wider the range of potentially viable solutions... the trick is to find people with different perspectives that usefully impinge on the problem at hand.'

So, build a diverse network of people who you trust and who get you, giving you options to turn to different people when you need to seek support or solace. We can't, however, ignore the attraction of confiding in strangers. The image of the drunk in the bar confiding all of their woes to an attentive barman is well known across the world but how genuine is it in reality?

I asked a number of the people I interviewed whether they would be comfortable opening up to strangers and the vast majority were insistent that they would not. I'm not so sure, however. I think there is something within us that likes the thought of opening up our deepest secrets and fears to people who we are confident we are unlikely to see again. We might not be looking for their advice but may appreciate the opportunity to share without being judged and without it affecting a relationship that is important to us. Perhaps this explains the centuries-old power of the Catholic confessional.

Natalya Khornauhova is a tour guide and translator in Irkutsk, Siberia. Natalya told me, "After your family, the best confidant you can have is the one who is travelling next to you on a long train trip. In Russia we have big distances and we have long-distance trains, so you can travel five days in one compartment with a total stranger. People share their whole life story with these people, maybe because they are never going to meet them again."

10.

BEING SOCIAL

One of the biggest complaints you'll hear about how social media has changed the world is the 'curse' of oversharing. In fact, it seems to be hard to get the balance right. Some people will complain about their friends painting an unrealistic, sunny picture of their perfect lives on their timelines, for others social media is just too transparent. "There are some things you just keep to yourself," they'll exclaim. Often it's the same people making both complaints!

Personally, I tend to share more of my positive experiences rather than negative thoughts on my social media profiles. Not because I want to portray myself in a positive light – I hope I engage authentically online – but because that is what feels right for me. But I recognise that this isn't the right fit for everyone and I try to support people who share their struggles and doubts.

I must admit though that when I saw a picture of social media expert Claire Boyles lying in a hospital bed looking as white as the sheets that surrounded her, accompanied by a graphic description of the trauma she had been through, I felt that it might be a touch too much. It made me feel uncomfortable and I mentally switched off. I couldn't understand why someone would share their personal trauma so vividly.

Claire had contracted sepsis after a hospital misdiagnosis, leaving her seriously ill and in danger of losing her life. She found herself undergoing three surgeries in three months and spending a lot of time in hospital, isolated and frustrated.

Claire's posts over the following days and weeks continued to paint a vivid picture of her poor health and the nightmare that she and her then partner Lewis were going through. I hadn't moved away from my initial instinctive reaction and didn't engage to the level that I now wish I had.

Once I knew that I wanted to write this book, Claire's story and her reasons for sharing so explicitly were always going to be part of the narrative. What leads people to open up to that extent and would she be willing to do so again if needed?

'I Can't Support Someone if I Don't Know'

It felt natural to Claire to share her experience along the way with her friends and wider network through social media. Claire has been using social media professionally and personally for many years.

"It's a natural platform to me. The main motivation for me in sharing the bad as well as the good on social media is that I am 100% honest about who I am as a person, on social media or in real life. It is very important for me to not pick and choose what bits of my life I want to show people. Obviously professionally I want to show the best bits but I also think it's very important for the good of human beings to show more things that we find challenging."

I think it's very important for the good of human beings to show more things that we find challenging.

Facebook was the platform of choice for Claire's story. Twitter and LinkedIn are networks that Claire uses primarily for professional purposes, so it didn't feel appropriate to go into any level of detail on either platform about what she and Lewis were going through. But Facebook allowed Claire to connect with the people who cared about her.

"Without the support that I got from my Facebook friends I would not have coped with everything. It gave me a lifeline. I was stuck in a hospital bed, the only thing that gave me any sense of power or a way to handle the situation and get that love and support from people who cared about me was Facebook."

For Claire the help she received from her friends was key. It wasn't just about having a platform to seek sympathy and attention. The response that Claire received as a result of her posts was tangible. Sometimes it was moral support, at other times it was more practical.

"One of the big things with the way I was treated in the hospital was that nobody heard me; they dismissed what I had to say. I was surrounded by so many situations which started to erode my own sense of self-esteem and my own personal boundaries. It was really important to get an external input."

The Downside of Sharing

I asked a friend of mine who knows Claire professionally whether he had seen her updates during her health issues and what he made of them. He was very clear that he felt she had overshared and that it would stop him ever referring business to her. He told me that he knew that the clients to whom he would refer her would be uncomfortable with the level of sharing that Claire employed.

I asked Claire if she had experienced other responses like this. Did her friends, family or wider network make their discomfort known and, if so, how did it make her feel?

"I don't think there were any major close friends who unfriended me during the period but I was aware that a lot of people felt uncomfortable with what I was sharing and I was OK with that."

Claire is in no doubt about the importance of social media as part of her survival and recovery process. She is adamant that she wouldn't have coped without it. "I know for a fact that I wouldn't be alive today if I hadn't shared the way I shared. I wouldn't do anything differently because the way I shared on Facebook gave me a lifeline to hold on to."

Too Fat to Run

Claire isn't the only person I spoke to who found social media to be the ideal way to engage with a community who could support them. For Claire it was her friends and family through Facebook but others find solace in online communities of people facing the same or similar challenges to them.

When you first meet Julie Creffield you don't immediately assume that you are in the presence of one of the most influential athletes in her discipline in the world. She's a lovely person, a bright and chipper East Londoner often seen with a smile on her face and at the heart of the group. She's just not… 'athletic'.

Julie is, to put it delicately, a large woman. Not obese by any means but hardly slender. Sporting activity for her family growing up involved sitting around the television watching the football together at the weekend. Into her 20s the limit of Julie's exercise was dancing at clubs on her regular nights out.

Yet Julie has brought together a global community of women who are inspired by her to take up sport. She's an influencer who has been called in by Sport England, England Athletics and the UK Parliament. Global brands queue up for Julie's endorsement and she's spoken on stages around the world to spread her message about the power of sport.

How does an overweight party animal become so influential in the sporting arena?

It all began with the build-up to the 2012 Olympic Games in London. The British government wanted the Olympics to inspire a whole new generation of people to take up sport and Julie was one of the early success stories.

While working for a local authority in East London in 2004, pitching for the Games in nearby Stratford, one of Julie's colleagues invited her to join a fitness club she was setting up. She agreed to run a 3k race. Julie finished last and was so far off the pace that the organisers had packed up everything and gone home before she even reached the (by that point non-existent) finish line. The embarrassment kick-started Julie's obsession with running. But she had no access to any information or support.

"There were no blogs; the pictures in the magazines didn't look like me. For about five years I was entering races, not training for them. I was a mess. I was still partying hard. I'd have a race in two weeks' time and I'd be out raving instead of getting up and training. I just approached it in the wrong way.

"There was no one like me out there running. I thought that runners were slim. I thought if I ran enough I would become slim too. I was just so clueless about everything to do with health and fitness."

Despite the lack of information and her struggles, Julie decided that if London won the bid to host the Olympics in 2012 she would enter the London Marathon.

Running in the Dark

Julie didn't feel that her friends and family would take her running seriously and was very self-aware of her weight and appearance when running. "It's something I did in secret. I'd run after dark, I'd run in really secluded places. No one ever came to watch me."

Julie did write about her experiences though, starting a blog that would lead to a huge change in her life and in the way she and other people saw her.

"I decided to just call it what it is: 'The Fat Girl's Guide to Running'. When I started it was supposed to be humorous but over the years it got a bit more serious, a bit more political and sometimes, when I called brands out, less about me and more about the issues.

"I think that's how it got loads of followers because people realised that it wasn't just a training record of what I was up to. I asked why you couldn't get a running coat in a big size. Why race organisers gave you only three hours to complete a half marathon. All those issues that really affect many women in sport."

The Fat Girl's Guide to Running a Business

While this was happening Julie's personal life was in a mess. She had been made redundant the day after the Olympics started, her relationship broke down and she found herself a single mother living on unemployment benefit and in danger of losing her house.

Julie decided to work out how she could monetise the community she was building around her. She set a challenge on Twitter and found 16 women who wanted to commit to running their first marathon. Julie offered to coach them for a year for free, to prove to herself that she could do it, and eight of the group went on to achieve their goal.

Soon Julie had a brand that really caught on – 'Too Fat to Run'.

"I hurt my back picking up my daughter, went to the doctor and the doctor took one look at me. He didn't even read my notes. I told him that I had a bad back and he basically made up his mind that it was because I was fat.

"He said, 'Right, you're going to have to rest.' He gave me painkillers and told me to go away and come back if it didn't improve. I asked him, 'What about exercise?' He looked at me blankly. I told him, 'I've got a marathon in two weeks' time.' He kind of went 'sssss'. He said, 'You can't run a marathon, you're too fat.' He obviously didn't know that I'd been running for nearly ten years by that point. I was stunned by that response and when I posted it in my group other women told me that it had happened to them too.

"That's where the 'Too Fat to Run' slogan came from. It really shocked people. The industry couldn't see how I could get away with it. But I was able to because nobody ever gets offended by that unless they've not been fat. It's only the skinny people that hate it.

Life in The Clubhouse

"I realised it wasn't about me, it was about how I could help other women. Some bloggers who are similar to me can't believe how I've achieved my success. They don't get it because it's this exchange of value that actually isn't about money, it's about helping each other out."

Part of Julie's charm is her openness and honesty. She's very open with the women who are part of her online running club, The Clubhouse, and has shared all of her ups and downs. They meet at running events, stay at each other's houses.

"There are maybe 350 women in the group. The special thing is, somebody will go quiet for a while and someone else will notice and they will ask how that person is. A lot of the women suffer with depression or anxiety and they all know what's going on in each other's lives. It's not just about the running."

The special thing is, somebody will go quiet for a while and someone else will notice and they will ask how that person is.

That positive impact is clearly what drives Julie. "I remember getting an email from somebody in the States saying, 'I check your blog first thing every morning. I've been running for years and thought I was the only overweight runner out there. I had nobody to ask the questions that you'd be too scared to ask a proper runner, so I pretty much trained for my first marathon by myself.'

"It was that loneliness that had brought people together. The technology enables people to connect and they form like family. Within a week of joining the community women tell me how they cannot believe how safe the space is. They are sharing things they've never spoken about their whole life. They find it empowering, the freedom to be able to have an honest conversation that they wouldn't share with their closest friends."

Is Social Media a Positive Channel for Sharing?

The stories shared by Claire and Julie make a strong case for social media as an effective channel for sharing. Indeed, some people may find it much easier being completely open about their challenges from the safety of their keyboard than they would when they can see the whites of somebody else's eyes. There are some things you do need to consider though.

First of all, everyone has an opinion but that doesn't necessarily mean either that their opinion is correct or that what worked for them would work for you. Use social media to open up, to vent and to seek insight but take everything others say with a pinch of salt.

Everyone has an opinion but that doesn't necessarily mean either that their opinion is correct or that what worked for them would work for you.

Finding communities of like-minded people, like Julie's Clubhouse, may well give you more confidence in sharing, although sometimes you may choose to lurk in the background and watch the conversation, drawing strength from seeing that you're not alone.

But again, recognise that especially among a community focused on a particular topic, it is likely that there will be very opinionated people who will be forceful in expressing their ideas.

You also need to think about who you want to be online and how other people will perceive your updates. A personal conversation has the potential to be a lot more confidential and a lot less viral than a post on Facebook. We constantly hear stories of how people's social media updates have come back to haunt them later in their lives; a good rule of thumb is not to post anything online, irrespective of privacy settings, that you wouldn't want anybody else to see.

A personal conversation has the potential to be a lot more confidential and a lot less viral than a post on Facebook.

Before diving into the conversation online and joining such a community or posting much more honest and open updates, go through the questions we discussed in the previous chapter but this time with a focus on how you engage online.

- *What do you need to talk about?*

- *Why are you sharing it online?*

- *When is the right time to share?*

- *How much should you share?*

- *Where do you share (what platform, which community)?*

- *Who do you want to be online?*

Finally, I would urge you to see social media as another tool that enables you to be more open with your network and to seek help more easily. But please don't see it as a replacement for face-to-face conversation.

It is easy to hide behind a keyboard but real conversations are far more powerful and nuances in speech and body language so much more visible when we sit together and talk.

SECTION THREE
TAKING ACTION

11.

TAKING RESPONSIBILITY

In chapter 10 I talked about how exposed you can be to strong opinions when turning to social media for support and the importance of taking those opinions with a pinch of salt. This is true of all of the advice and support that you will receive once you are open to asking for help.

Ultimately, you are responsible for the direction of your own life and the success of your career or business. It makes absolute sense to seek different ideas, perspectives and opinions but it is important that you have a filter through which to receive those inputs.

The output – the action you take – should be wholly owned by you.

And there does need to be an output. The first three sections of this book represent the obstacles that lie in the path of seeking help and support from others. Many of us lack the courage to be uncomfortable and expose what we perceive to be our weaknesses.

Even if we can find the courage, we lack a strategy, a clear direction, to help us to do so effectively.

Once we have processed and understood our emotions and considered the best approach, we still need to take the plunge and take action. And that, probably, is the hardest hurdle of all to overcome.

Once we have processed and understood our emotions and considered the best approach, we still need to take the plunge and take action.

Other people can help you on your way and make it easier for you to share but only one person has responsibility for making that happen.

You.

In chapter 1 we saw how Billy Schwer let his life go off the rails after losing his world boxing crown. It took a couple of years but Billy took responsibility for getting his life back on track and taking the action needed to really turn things around.

The boxer, standing alone in the ring, with his or her corner shouting directions while they get jabbed time and again in the face, provides a striking metaphor for how we overcome our challenges in life. The team in the corner is important but you are the one who is sticking their chin out and trying to avoid getting knocked down.

"A corner can win you the fight," Billy told me. "When they are looking at the fight from outside the ring, they can see opportunities that you cannot see. But then, when you are in such an intense environment, it is very difficult to implement what they see and take action. You are the only person who you can rely on. You have got a team around you but you go in there and you're fighting on your own."

Review, Reframe and Respond

Fortunately, many of the issues we face in life and work give us a lot more time to react than a world-class boxer will enjoy in the ring. There are three stages that you need to go through when taking advice on board and working out how to process and act on it.

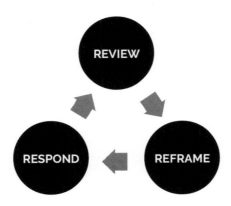

First of all, we need to *review* the information we have been given. Depending on the nature of the challenge, you may want to seek advice from a range of different people with different perspectives. The more complex the issue, the more you need to understand all of the potential ramifications.

If, for example, you are making major public policy decisions, you wouldn't simply ask for the advice of a mentor or friend. You'll need to invite opinions from a range of people who have an interest in the outcome of the policy discussion and try to ensure that all possibilities are mapped before finalising your way forward. We'll see what happens if you don't seek enough input in chapter 19.

Other decisions, such as whether to put yourself forward for a promotion, or how to approach a potential client, will probably need a lower degree of scrutiny and fewer conversations with different people before you make a decision. Take on board what other people say and, if you can, listen initially without prejudging your position. The more objective you can be with each individual perspective, the better you will be able to weigh up each argument on its individual merits and come to a balanced and informed conclusion.

The more objective you can be with each individual perspective, the better you will be able to weigh up each argument on its individual merits and come to a balanced and informed conclusion.

Remember that in many circumstances, both professional and personal, people will have their own agenda and beliefs that influence their counsel.

Once we have reviewed the advice that we have received, we then need to *reframe* it, to challenge the assumptions we have made and test different scenarios. How important is the likely action in the grand scheme of things and how will you benefit from taking it?

When filtering advice, ask yourself not just how right the advice sounds to you but how seamlessly you can implement it. What are the likely repercussions? Again, remember that it's you who is taking final responsibility, so you need to be clear in your mind about what the likely outcomes of that course of action will be.

It's not as simple as taking in every different opinion and then weighing up which side of the debate is more popular. As the person taking responsibility, you need to be comfortable with the final decision.

Listen to your gut. How do you feel about the final decision? Deep down you know what you most want to do and your intuition is designed to guide you to the decision that you feel more comfortable with. There's a lot of noise designed to drown out that instinct and we need to tune in to our real feelings and help them to inform our final choice, alongside the advice we have taken.

I like the idea of finding what our instinct tells us by making decisions by the toss of a coin. Call 'heads' or 'tails' and then see how you feel when the coin lands. If you are happy with the outcome, you will know that it's the right decision. If not, change it.

Understand the perspective from which advice was offered. If it's based on the experience of the person offering solutions, how similar were the circumstances they faced to yours? If the context was completely different, then how effectively will that same action play out if you applied it?

Understand the perspective from which advice was offered. If the context was completely different, then how effectively will that same action play out if you applied it?

Listen to and review the advice, see it from the lens of your own circumstances and preferences, then make a decision that is appropriate to you. You may take on board the suggestions of your network wholly, you make take elements and adapt the advice to suit your unique issue, or you may discard them completely and choose another route.

Finally, once you have weighed up and contextualised the advice from your corner, you need to *respond* and take action. You need to throw some punches of your own.

During a fight the bell rings every three minutes to give the boxers a rest and to allow their respective corners to patch them up and remind them of the game plan, as well as to adapt that plan to changes in circumstances, such as a cut above the eye or a broken nose.

Similarly, you don't need to be left alone once you have taken advice from your own corner. You can agree a game plan, go back between rounds for them to hold you accountable and constantly review your approach depending on your progress.

Commitment and accountability lie at the core of taking effective action.

Commitment and accountability lie at the core of taking effective action.

The next step is to identify who stands in that corner. And while you might speak to a range of people informally, there are also plenty of ways to formalise that relationship and make sure the accountability sticks. Over the next two chapters I want to explore two such methods.

12.

MASTERMINDING

There are many ways to tap into a strong support network, from informal calls to ask for advice to formal mentoring arrangements. One of the most powerful ways to seek such support is mastermind groups.

Napoleon Hill first brought the concept of 'Master Mind Groups' to the public attention in his book *Think and Grow Rich* in 1938[8]. More recently, in his book *The Start Up of You*[9], Reid Hoffman shares the story of Joseph Priestley, a young amateur scientist who, in 1765, was running experiments in a makeshift laboratory in the English countryside.

Hoffman explains that Priestley, 'Was exceptionally bright but isolated from any peers, until one December day when he travelled into London to attend the Club of Honest Whigs. Benjamin Franklin, who was in England promoting the interests of the

American colonies, convened his big thinking friends at the London Coffee House on alternating Thursdays.

'Priestley attended to get feedback on a book idea about scientists' progress on understanding electricity. He got much more than feedback. Franklin and his friends swelled in support of Priestley; they offered to open their private scientific libraries to him. They offered to review drafts of his manuscript. They offered their friendship and encouragement. Crucially Priestley reciprocated all the way.

'In short, Priestley's night at the coffeehouse dramatically altered the trajectory of his career. Priestley went from semi-isolation to plugging into an existing network of relationships and collaborations that the coffee house environment facilitated. He went on to have an illustrious scientific and writing career, famously discovering the existence of oxygen.'

In short, Priestley's night at the coffeehouse dramatically altered the trajectory of his career. Priestley went from semi-isolation to plugging into an existing network of relationships and collaborations that the coffee house environment facilitated.

Mastermind groups have been an important tool in the development of my own business. In many of my talks I share the story of how advice from one such group helped prevent our business from sliding into disaster and, instead, supported us in making a very brave decision to write off big losses and turn the venture around into something very different.

I have been, and remain, involved in mastermind groups with fellow entrepreneurs and fellow professional speakers, all of which have been instrumental in the growth of our business.

Within some of my workshops I run a 'Five-Minute Mini-Mastermind' and it's been incredible to witness the power of bringing groups of people together at random, with no notice or preparation time, to address a challenge and find solutions. Not one group has ever found the session without value and they remain one of the most popular parts of my workshops.

If mastermind groups can have such an impact when put together in such a random way, just how powerful could they be if you focused your attention on getting the most out of them? Here are my top ten steps to help you get just that value.

1. The right ingredients

The success of mastermind groups is heavily reliant on the right mix of people within its ranks. If the abilities and experience of the participants are too broad, you will find some people questioning the value the group can bring to them, while others lose confidence in the value they can bring to the group.

The success of mastermind groups is heavily reliant on the right mix of people within its ranks.

The best mastermind group is one where everyone brings equal value, in one way or another. Everyone needs to be able to both contribute to and gain from the experience.

While it's almost impossible to ensure equal contributions across the board, look to bring together people who are at similar stages in their career or business journey. You might look for people who run businesses in the same field (as mastermind groups of professional speakers and also within the fitness industry do) or who are in a similar role within the same company or industry. Alternatively, you can mix up people who have expertise in different areas, such as marketing, finance, management and technology.

Ideally, individual members of the group will all know each other first. If you're bringing together a group of people who you know but who don't know each other, try to match people who are likely to have things in common and arrange for them to meet socially first to ensure that the chemistry will work.

If you are bringing together people who don't know each other, give them time and space to get to know, like and trust each other before expecting full transparency and mutual support. You want people to be comfortable sticking together; you don't want to keep on bringing in new members on a regular basis, as trust and rapport aren't allowed to develop.

2.   A shared vision

It helps if you know what you're doing there! Everyone needs to think about why he or she is joining and what success will look like. Perhaps you want your mastermind group to help you achieve a desired promotion, win projects in a new industry or take your business to a new level.

You then need to share those goals and ask yourself both whether the objectives are mutually compatible and also how you can best structure the group to meet everyone's.

A clear vision of success will make each participant's commitment to the group easier to make and help you to retain focus as the group develops. Don't be frightened to revisit the objectives and ask whether they are being met.

A clear vision of success will make each participant's commitment to the group easier to make.

That may lead to a change in approach, a change in objectives or even sometimes a change in the makeup of the group. But a mastermind group can only truly add value if everyone buys into making it a success.

3. Commitment

Depending on your format, the numbers in a mastermind group need to be fairly low compared to other networking events. I believe that the ideal number is around six people. If you restrict your membership to that number, you need a high level of commitment to attend.

In one group there was a much larger pool of members with a lower commitment to attend, meaning that you might see different people and get a different perspective each time. While that approach has its merits, all too often we would see people only turn up when they had a challenge and then disappear once they have their answers.

A smaller group enables both stronger levels of trust to be developed and also a greater understanding over time of each other's business and individual challenges. Accountability increases and the questioning and subsequent solutions proposed are based on that greater understanding. Agree the frequency of meetings, something that everyone can commit to but allows you to maintain a positive momentum at the same time.

4.   A clear agenda

Agree on an agenda for meetings that is designed to best meet the objectives the group has set. I suggest appointing a chair for each meeting, and rotating the responsibility to plan and take control of the agenda.

You will need to find the right balance of allowing everyone in the group to have some 'air time' to share challenges and update their fellow members, and setting aside enough time to look at particular challenges in depth.

While the five minutes allowed for my mini-mastermind session in my workshops produces some great results, there is no doubt that this really isn't enough time to offer more than the most basic understanding and suggestions. In some groups I have been in each member has had around 45 minutes for their own challenge, while in others we have concentrated a much longer period of time on just one or two people. You have to work out which is the right balance for you.

Whatever time you allocate to each challenge, the format that works best in my experience is as follows:

- The person with the challenge outlines the support they are looking for, together with explaining the background.

- The rest of the group then asks questions. Their objective during this period is research – they should be looking to get to an understanding of the problem or identifying if there is a greater underlying issue that the person with the challenge is not aware of or opening up to.

- The person with the challenge then restates their question. This allows them to change their challenge if questioning has opened up a related issue, or to bring their inquisitors back on track if they feel they have strayed.

- The rest of the group then offers suggestions and solutions. The person with the challenge can only respond by saying 'Thank you.' There should be no defensive response; they need to be open to new ideas. I'll explain why this is so important in step nine.

5. Be prepared

You need to be fully prepared if you are going to take away the best ideas from your peers. Sometimes that also means preparing them.

Set some time aside before your meetings to remind yourself why you are going and what you want to achieve. There is a high investment in terms of time and energy involved, so you have to ensure you have the best chance of a substantial return.

Before each meeting ask yourself what your biggest challenges are at the moment and what support you would be most likely to benefit from. If you can't think of anything, try again. I struggle to believe that anyone is in such a wonderful position in his or her career or business that they wouldn't benefit from some advice, feedback or a different perspective.

If everything is going well, how could you find that extra 10% to make it even better? How do you identify what it is you're doing so that you can keep on doing it or even improve?

If you really can't see how the group can add value to your journey, are you in the right group?

If everything is going well, how could you find that extra 10% to make it even better?

6. Chatham House Rule

It's vitally important (particularly with step seven in mind) that every member of the group has complete faith that they can speak openly, confident that what they say won't be shared elsewhere. That means complete trust between members, something that may take time to establish.

Amateur rugby players will be aware of the concept of 'what goes on tour stays on tour', while others may be more familiar with the Chatham House Rule[10].

In masterminding terms, the intention is that everything is shared in strict confidentiality and, I would suggest, goes further to state none of the information shared should be used without the clear permission of the originator. It would be advisable that, as a group, you should agree on your own understanding of what is confidential and how information shared within the group can be used elsewhere and how this impacts any policy of inviting visitors and prospective members to your meetings.

7. Total honesty

With Chatham House Rule in place and strong levels of trust between participants, members of your mastermind group should now feel comfortable being completely open and transparent. It's important to have a safe haven to turn to when we need support and advice.

If you don't open up, the group can't do its job. I've been in groups where we've found out that a fellow member was in trouble when it was already too late to help them. If they had been more honest at an earlier stage, the group could have done its job.

8. Searching questions

When a member of your mastermind group starts presenting their challenge, it's tempting to see the answer straight away and the urge starts to build up to intervene and put the world to rights. Please resist.

More often than not you will be able to provide a better solution if you investigate the issue in more detail first. Before any solutions are presented, members of the group should do their research, asking questions designed to find out what has been done before, what has or hasn't worked, whether alternatives have been considered and much more.

More often than not you will be able to provide a better solution if you investigate the issue in more detail first.

If you have a solution in mind, ask questions that will help you test whether that really is the right approach. And look to see whether the challenge presented is the true issue holding your colleague back.

I mentioned earlier how a mastermind group helped to turn around our business. The advice I requested was how to market ourselves more effectively. After the right questioning it turned out that the challenge was unrelated to marketing. My heart wasn't in the business and without my conviction it was destined to fail, however we presented it.

As a result of the right questioning the group changed their focus and helped me to identify what I really did want to do and what I needed to focus on to make a change in direction a success.

9. An open mind

One of the golden rules of masterminding is that your only response to any suggested solutions should be 'Thank you'. A mastermind group gives you access to different perspectives and approaches and you need to harness that advantage.

One of the golden rules of masterminding is that your only response to any suggested solutions should be 'Thank you'.

The biggest barrier to you doing so is you.

We all seem to have a little voice in the corner of our minds that, as soon as something is suggested, jumps in to tell us why it won't work. Saying 'Thank you' quietens the little voice immediately and buys you time to process the suggestion and work out the impact it would have on your challenge.

You need an open mind. The chance to consider ideas you wouldn't previously have given time to. Once you have processed the ideas from your session you can go back and test them further with the group but initially pause and allow yourself to process them first.

10. Accountability

A mastermind group isn't there just to provide each other with ideas and suggestions. As mentioned earlier, they should be supportive of each other and challenging too.

After their session, each member should commit to their follow-up and share it with their peers. Set dates by which actions will be taken. Maybe even appoint a 'buddy' from within the group to chase them up. At following meetings take some time to ask for feedback and review progress. Allow some time to reconsider the approach if needed.

And allow for celebrations after the meeting when all the support provided has led to a challenge surmounted and a business or career reaching another successful landmark.

13.

MENTORING

One of the more traditional approaches to asking for help in a formal setting is getting a mentor or coach. A mentor has experience of the journey you are facing or has the expertise you are lacking and guides you with the benefit of that experience. A coach does not necessarily have the insights you need but they have the skillset to help you find the answers for yourself.

In this chapter I want to focus on mentoring relationships but many of the ideas I share are equally applicable if you choose to work with a coach. At the time of writing I have a coach, a mentor and two mastermind groups, as well as a range of people who fill those roles informally. So, it doesn't have to be one or the other.

Whatever you do choose, the point I stressed in chapter 11 about you taking personal responsibility for the ultimate decision stands.

What is a Mentor?

The Irish speaker and expert on high trust relationships, Sean Weafer, describes a mentor as 'someone who can transfer role-specific skills or knowledge that helps the mentee accelerate their development'.

I look to a mentor as someone with whom I can share ideas and get brutally honest feedback. My mentor fits the persona of my ideal clients for a lot of my work, so when I come up with new ideas for that market or new marketing to promote them, I can share them with him. If they don't resonate with him, there is a good chance that they won't hit the mark with potential clients.

But a mentor is not just a sounding board. I always look for someone who can give me clear advice, challenge my convictions and hold me accountable for what I have promised to do. A good mentoring relationship is also an effective way to lift your head away from the day-to-day pressures of your role and force you to look at how your career or business are developing over the long term.

A mentor is not just a sounding board. I always look for someone who can give me clear advice, challenge my convictions and hold me accountable for what I have promised to do.

I have mentioned the differences between a mentor and a coach. To help avoid further confusion, it's worth mentioning the third type of person who can play a key role in your career development and that's a sponsor.

A sponsor is typically somebody more senior within your own organisation who will proactively advocate for your promotion, often to a specific role. A sponsor may advise you and guide you to make sure you are ready for that role and worthy of their advocacy, but they will generally be less invested in your long-term career planning and the detail than a mentor.

While there may be some exceptions, mentors don't normally focus on teaching technical skills. Their approach is more likely to be strategic initially, looking at what you want to achieve and how you plan to get there, followed by suggesting some tactics. I would expect a mentor to suggest tactics for me to consider but not necessarily teach me how to implement them.

One exception might be a reverse mentoring relationship, particularly one focused on new technology and social media. Because of the focus on experience, mentors are often perceived to be grey haired and towards the end of their career. This is an out of date image anyway, many people start mentoring in their 40s or even earlier. But reverse mentoring is growing as senior executives turn to younger generations to help them understand the changing workplace and the technology that serves it.

The age or seniority of your mentor is not the most important thing. The two key factors are their ability to guide you and their willingness to do so.

What are the Qualities You Want in Your Mentor?

Over the years I have talked about mentoring in presentations for a range of organisations across the world. While most of those organisations offer a formal mentoring programme to their staff, sadly I have found that many of these programmes are ineffective. There is a lack of awareness of their existence and often a small pool of volunteers to mentor others.

While some mentoring schemes are set up cleverly to work out how to match each person to the right mentor, in many cases the process seems somewhat random. If you're not paired with the right person, the chances of the relationship being sustainable, let alone useful and productive, are substantially diminished.

Do your planning and research first. If there is a formal company mentoring scheme available to you, include that in your research. But don't simply delegate responsibility for finding the right mentor wholly to your company's HR department or the person who volunteered to run the scheme. Even if you do go down that route, you need to give them very clear guidelines about what you are looking for.

Which means that you need to know. It doesn't serve you to set generic objectives. Looking for 'somebody to help me to progress my career' is not going to help you identify your ideal mentor. The more specific you can be about what you need to achieve, the more clearly you will be able to identify the ideal person to support you.

The more specific you can be about what you need to achieve, the more clearly you will be able to identify the ideal person to support you.

I approached the mentor I am working with now because of his experience in buying and selling businesses. My strong personal relationship with him and trust in his knowledge and experience were also key factors for me. But his professional expertise stood out.

I'm not looking to either buy a new business or sell my existing one but I do want my business to grow. I need somebody to support me who can guide and cajole me into doing what I dislike and don't find natural – being a businessman. And who better to do that than somebody with the experience of buying and selling multiple businesses?

Ask yourself these questions:

- Where do I want to be in the next five or ten years?

- What needs to happen first?

- What is stopping me from getting there?

- What challenges do I struggle with the most?

Once you know the answers to these questions, you can then ask yourself:

- Who do I know who has achieved what I am looking to achieve, ideally from a similar starting point?

- Who do I trust and respect?

- Who will challenge me robustly?

Your mentor needs to be objective, so avoid people who are in your direct line of management or colleagues with whom you have to work closely. Ideally, they will have a good understanding of your environment and challenges without being directly involved.

I would also suggest looking for somebody who shares similar values to you, who you admire and respect not just for what they have achieved but also for the way in which they achieved it. Similar values do not always equate to taking a similar approach. It's fine to find a mentor who will think differently and challenge the way you do things. In many ways it's more than fine, it's desirable.

It's fine to find a mentor who will think differently and challenge the way you do things. In many ways it's more than fine, it's desirable.

Think laterally. Prospective mentors may have been on a similar journey but in a different field. Having perspectives from varying industries or backgrounds could provide just the type of challenge and disruptive thought that you need.

Finally, should you like your mentor? I would argue that as long as you don't actively dislike them it isn't important. It's far more important that you respect them. If you are too close, it's possible they won't challenge you enough or you won't take their advice seriously.

Make sure that if you do have a strong relationship you can separate what is said in mentoring sessions from your day-to-day engagement.

How Do You Find the Right Mentor?

I would always start looking for a mentor by looking to my own network. Who do I know who has the qualities I've identified in my search for a mentor and who may be willing to support me?

If I don't know anyone personally who fits the bill, I'd then look to people whose reputation I'm aware of and admire. I'd look for potential role models within my own organisation (through the internal mentoring programme, by asking my line manager or through a request to HR as well as by personal approach); across my industry and, as mentioned previously, people who have the right kind of experience or insight but in a different sphere.

My next step, if I'm still struggling, would be to approach people I trust and ask them for recommendations and introductions. You can also approach speakers and influencers at industry events and conferences but bear in mind that if they don't know you, they may not be as likely to accede to a request out of the blue. Approach them with a view to building the relationship first and ask at the right moment.

Once you have identified who you would like to mentor you, ask them. Recognise that they might say no, and that is perfectly OK. In fact, make sure that when you ask them they do not feel under pressure to say yes. A mentoring relationship will only work if both parties are keen.

There are many reasons why people might turn you down and very few of them are to do with you. It is quite possible that people won't agree to mentor you because they are too busy, because they don't feel confident about how they can support you (it is important for you to be really clear about what you expect) or because they don't really know you.

There are many reasons why people might turn you down and very few of them are to do with you.

If you don't take rejection personally, it makes it a lot easier to ask people and then, if you have to, move on. I've had more than one person say no to me, maybe because the people I ask are very successful and very busy. I know that I'm still on very good terms with all of them and they respect me and what I do.

The Mentoring Relationship

Kerrie Dorman, Founder of the Association of Business Mentors, summed up the foundations of a strong mentoring relationship perfectly when she told me, "A mentoring relationship can be either formal or informal. Either way, boundaries have to be highlighted and adhered to. The relationship is a team effort; transparency, honesty and regular reviews are essential."

The core ingredients of a strong, formal mentoring relationship are:

1. *Clarity of purpose* - Both parties need to be clear about what you are trying to achieve and how you plan to get there. Expectations of each other should be set at the very beginning and maintained.

2. *Driven by the mentee* - This is particularly important in the case of an unpaid mentoring relationship. Why should your mentor be invested in the relationship if you're not? They are investing their time, experience and expertise.

3. *Honesty and transparency* - This should come from both sides; a mentoring relationship won't work if the mentee fails to be completely open about the challenges they are facing or if the mentor sugarcoats the advice they give.

4. *Curiosity and a willingness to explore* - Leave behind preconceived ideas of what you are going to do and a desire for your mentor to rubber stamp it. Be open to new ideas, even ones which you have previously written off.

5. *Accountability* - A great mentor doesn't just give advice but agrees actions going forward and challenges their mentee to make sure that those actions are either followed through or the reasons why not are explored and challenged.

6.   *Leave your ego at the door* - You are not there to impress each other but to seek or give help. A note to mentors: your experience is valuable but you are best positioned to help and support others when you make the conversation about them and not about you.

Mentoring may be a relationship but it's not a marriage. While some mentoring relationships might last for years, many reach a natural conclusion after a period of time. New challenges might require new insights; familiarity may breed contempt or, indeed, breed friendships which move the conversations on to a different plane.

Be open to recognise when the mentoring relationship has served its purpose. Some people favour setting a fixed term on mentoring relationships; I believe that each one is different so that is not always appropriate. It's fine, however, to review progress on a regular basis.

Pay it Forward

We will look at helping others to open up and seek support over the course of the next few chapters, but it would be remiss to focus on mentoring without urging you to make yourself available to mentor others.

Unless provided as a paid-for service, most mentoring relationships are, by their very nature, one-way in terms of value provided. That is fine and usually works on the unspoken understanding that the mentee will pay it forward. That might be later in your career but it could be sooner than you think.

Understand what you have to offer now, there's likely to be someone who would benefit. List out your experience, expertise and skillsets and ask yourself who in your network might value those resources. As we're about to explore, you don't need to just wait to be asked, you can create the opportunity yourself to support others.

Section Four

Inspiring and Enabling Vulnerability in Others

14.

BEING THERE...
AS A FRIEND

My primary objective in writing this book has always been to inspire you to be more confident to open up and ask for help. We are all, however, reliant on the right support networks and environment being in place to enable us to truly be vulnerable. It simply won't benefit you to take my advice if you live and work in a toxic, non-supportive culture where you could be penalised for doing so.

Over the course of this section I want to explore the role we play in creating positive environments where people feel safe sharing, whether as individuals, as leaders or as organisations.

How different might things have been for Leon Mackenzie if the management and coaches at the clubs he played for had made him feel that being vulnerable would not negatively impact his place in the team? Would Dawnna St Louis have found herself contemplating suicide if the adults charged with being there for her had supported and encouraged her?

When you look back at the stories I have shared on this journey, it is striking how much support there was for the people who needed it. From the wisdom and openness of Leonard Cohen and Tom Petty when Hattie Webb suffered from anxiety attacks, through the Girl Scout leader who took Pegine and her rival gang members under her wing, to the online communities who supported Kelly, Claire and, in the case of the plus size runners, each other.

My second objective in writing this book is to ensure that you pay it forward. That you seek to help and support your network in the same way that you will be looking for others who can support you.

Fighting Fear

Supporting others is not as simple as inviting them to share with you. It is good for us to know that others are willing to listen, support and advise, but look at your own mindset and experience and you will probably recognise various reasons for resistance that have stopped you from sharing even when invited to do so. The people around you are no different.

Supporting others is not as simple as inviting them to share with you.

We need to create the space for others to share. That begins with understanding their starting point.

Andy Agathangelou, who changed his relationship with vulnerability when forced to by his need to make his Transparency Taskforce a success (chapter 7), believes that ultimately the issues within the financial services sector, where he operates, are driven by fear. Fear of sales people missing targets. Fear for people's job security and future. Fear of missing out on a promotion or a bonus.

"A fear mindset is dangerous," Andy told me. "When people are scared, they will do things that are not right. Rejection is a really powerful emotional experience.

"There are many people who have learned to not ask for help because they have been let down or disappointed before. We as a society need to become better at recognising that somebody asking for help is very likely to be worthy of receiving it. That is why, whenever somebody asks me for help, I try to find that good part in me that says 'this person probably did not want to ask for help'. But the fact that someone is asking for help means that there should be a predisposition to reach out to give them the help that they need."

I don't think that Andy's observations are true just for the financial services sector. We talked a lot about the various reasons why we don't ask for help in section one of the book and fear underpins a lot of them – fear of looking foolish, of seeming weak and ineffective.

Fear of being let down needs to be on that list too. We need to let people know that they can trust us. When people do confide in us, it is important that we listen with intent, focused fully on them and their challenges. Even if we can't help them, they need to feel listened to and understood.

When people do confide in us, it is important that we listen with intent, focused fully on them and their challenges. Even if we can't help them, they need to feel listened to and understood.

One of my biggest failings in conversation is my tendency to equate what someone is sharing with me with my own experience. If they start to tell me about their holiday in Morocco, I'll tell them when I went there. If they talk about their favourite band, film or cuisine, I'll jump in with my own opinion (and I'm very opinionated!).

It's not just me, it's a common trait to find ground in a conversation where we are comfortable. And we're comfortable with what we are familiar with. That might be fine, to a degree, in day-to-day small talk. But when somebody is sharing a major challenge with you, the focus should be on them. If your experiences of similar issues are relevant and will help them to either find a solution or feel less isolated, share by all means. But don't necessarily lead with that, understand before contributing.

The more people feel listened to and respected, the more they will feel comfortable and open up. Understand when people are asking for advice and when they are just looking to vent, looking for comfort. Once they overcome the fear of sharing and being judged for doing so, then people will share more willingly and openly and you can make a tremendous difference to their lives.

Semantic Differential Questioning

Sometimes you sense, or even know, that somebody needs help and support but they are just not asking. How do you encourage them to open up?

Ivan Misner told me that he uses a particular technique to shift conversations from a courteous exchange to something more meaningful where he feels it's needed.

"If you really want to know how someone is, you use a technique called Semantic Differential Questioning. You ask them the same question two or three times.

'How are you doing?'

'I'm doing good, I'm doing fine.'

'No really, how are you doing?'

'Yeah things are OK.'

'No Andy really, I really want to know, how are you?'

"I swear to you, you get a different answer on number three.

"It's like people put up a wall but the wall is made out of Styrofoam. It's just enough to block you but it's actually pretty easy to get through if they really feel comfortable with you. I see women do this way better than men. I've been in a conversation with two guys when one of them has said 'I just found out I have a heart condition' to which the other replied 'Oh God, I'm sorry to hear that. Hey how about those Dodgers this weekend?' They bypass it.

"Just be a friend, but you can't be that friend if you don't have the conversation."

It's Not About You

In chapter 9 I introduced you to Kelly and looked at the impact on her life of losing twin daughters and how she coped. What I didn't tell you was that I was with Kelly when it happened.

It was a beautiful day. The sun was shining and we were laid out in Hyde Park enjoying ice creams while KC and the Sunshine Band urged us to 'Shake Your Booty' and insisted 'That's the Way I Like It'.

Kelly was looking happier and more relaxed than I had seen her for a long time. Lee and Kelly had been trying for a baby for several years. She had suffered a miscarriage a couple of years before and she and Lee were on their third round of IVF. This time it was good news, Kelly was four months pregnant and it was twins.

We finished our ice creams and Kelly left me to head behind the main stage to use the toilets. About 15 minutes after Kelly disappeared my phone rang. It was Kelly and she spoke quickly and in a panicked voice. "You need to come quickly, the babies are coming."

The rest of the afternoon until late in the evening were spent in a St John's medical tent, in the back of an ambulance and finally in hospital. Kelly had given birth to one of the twins straight away and was terrified for her second child. Lee is a wedding photographer and was working; it wasn't until late that we could even let him know what was happening, let alone for him to get to Kelly's side.

I stood next to Kelly's bed holding her hand and feeling utterly powerless. I didn't know what to do or what to say. There was nothing I could say to comfort her. If there was, I had no idea what those magic words were. I can't remember a more traumatic day and I have never felt so lacking in any ability to make a difference. I wanted to change events, I wanted to reassure Kelly, I wanted to take the pain away but I could do none of that. I felt completely useless.

Talking to Kelly a couple of years afterwards she told me that I had been a big help, just being there. I didn't have to say anything, in fact when I did, I'm pretty sure it wasn't that constructive.

My obsession with what I could do to help was misplaced. I was looking to provide a solution, to create the change. But I wasn't in any position to do so. I couldn't make things better and I couldn't change what was happening. All I could do was be there for her. And sometimes that's all it takes. Creating the space for people to open up and be vulnerable isn't always about you being able to provide the solutions and save the day.

I couldn't make things better and I couldn't change what was happening. All I could do was be there for her. And sometimes that's all it takes.

Yes, sometimes you might. And at other times you could potentially make introductions to others who are better placed than you.

But it all begins with you just being there and letting people feel safe with you.

15.

BEING THERE...
AS A LEADER

When Ronnie's wife moved out of their home and out of his life, he felt confused and scared; the life he had known for over 20 years was over and he didn't know what was next. He was very quiet at work the following week. People noticed a change in him and he told his closest colleagues that his wife had left him but that he didn't really want to talk about it.

Phil Jones, the CEO of the company he worked for, asked Ronnie to do something for him. Ronnie told him that he didn't feel in the right frame of mind because of a situation at home and Phil suggested that he come up to his office for a chat.

"We sat down in his office and I told him everything," Ronnie explained. "Phil being the type of guy that he is absolutely couldn't help me enough. He never butted in once, which I found amazing. I'd never spoken to him on that sort of level before."

Phil was the first person to whom Ronnie had opened up. He hadn't told anyone in his family, not even his mother. Phil just sat there and listened, letting Ronnie pour his heart out. Ronnie found it easy talking to Phil despite the fact that Phil was the CEO of the company.

"I didn't want to tell anybody anything, but within a week I was in his office and I was telling him everything. I know he's my boss but also he is a good leader. And he's a great guy as well. Phil is always inquiring, always asking."

Phil Jones MBE has worked for Brother UK for over 25 years, becoming Managing Director in 2013, around the same time that Ronnie Cavanagh's wife left him. Phil is the perfect example of how a business leader can be strong and purposeful but encourage vulnerability at the same time. In fact, it was Phil who suggested that I speak to Ronnie when I interviewed him for this book.

Phil told me that creating the right culture was one of his leading priorities when he took the top job. "What I wanted to do was to really capture the good stuff and start cutting away the things that don't matter anymore. I wanted to build a culture based around something called alacrity, which basically means a happy state of readiness.

"Happy that we can all come to work, happy that we love our jobs and we are actually happy as people. But at the same time the state of readiness to perform against the external market conditions which are fast moving, so we need to be adaptable to those conditions.

"A key component to our culture is *at your side*, which is our global strapline: 'Brother at Your Side'. That comes to life in being at the side of each other. We're at the side of our customer, that's the external facing element, but internally it also means how do you care for me? How do I care for you? Am I at your side?

"I realised many years ago that instead of just grinding processes, you need to give people permission to be themselves. You as the leader show the characteristics that demonstrate what it is you are trying to encourage. Compassion, for example. Care, that you apply at an excellent level yourself."

I realised many years ago that instead of just grinding processes, you need to give people permission to be themselves.

Phil's support for Ronnie demonstrates the power of the caring culture he has tried to instil at Brother UK. And it's clear that the conversation impacted Phil almost as much as it did Ronnie.

"I think we spent nearly five hours together over two or three sessions. What he says about what that moment did for him just shows me that your words are so powerful when chosen correctly. If you've got knowledge and you've got belief that you can help people, wow! Workplace performance is all about that."

Keeping it Real

Creating the right environment for people to share begins with leaders setting the right example, being willing to both be vulnerable and encourage others to do so. Once those foundations are in place, challenges – however big – become much easier to cope with and communicate.

Creating the right environment for people to share begins with leaders setting the right example, being willing to both be vulnerable and encourage other people to do so.

Phil Gardner joined the main board of travel company Thomas Cook in October 2018 as Sales and e-Commerce Director after three years with the company. From day one, Phil was careful to ensure that he didn't set himself above his team or any of his colleagues.

"One of the things that I did really early on was to openly admit that I didn't have all the answers," he told me. "'I don't know' isn't a popular thing to say but quite often an appropriate one."

On 23 September 2019, a day that Phil says will be forever etched in his memory as one of the worst days of his life, the relationships and trust that Phil had developed with his team came to the fore.

After weeks of much publicised struggle to remain afloat, Thomas Cook finally gave up the fight and the company was liquidated. That morning Phil had to read out the names of the 201 members of his team, one by one, with a liquidator stood next to him, and 195 of them were sent home without pay. They weren't even paid for the three weeks of the month they had worked to that point.

Phil told me, "I think that the open approach, being honest at a time of such devastation, is one of the few things you have in your arsenal. I distinctly remember having about a 30-minute window before we had to stand up and brief all our colleagues.

"During that window I went round as many people as I could and advised them that it was going to be a really difficult day, that it was going to be brutal emotionally. At that point, the one thing that I found myself holding on to was a desire to try and maintain some modicum of integrity. And I think being honest about what's in front of you is the only thing you've got left at that point."

It was here that Phil recognised the importance of the relationships he had been developing in the time he had been with Thomas Cook and the open culture he had encouraged in the department.

"I found that, while the news was not easy to deliver emotionally, I knew it would be well received. It was in keeping with the consistent approach that we've had as a department for some time."

Despite the trauma of the day and the devastation caused, Phil experienced a lot less pushback than might have been expected. "I was trying to allow people the opportunity to speak openly at a time when I knew that they still could. I had a lot of really lovely comments about how much that was appreciated by people at the time."

I was trying to allow people the opportunity to speak openly at a time when I knew that they still could.

Throughout the whole experience, it was important for Phil to stay strong so that he could offer reassurance to the people for whom he was responsible. Eventually, however, the mask cracked.

"I thought it was important to keep it together. I'd say that at least half of the people in the building were crying. Part of it was the emotion of not seeing something coming, part of it was the realisation of not having an income and not knowing how you're going to pay the mortgage.

"I really tried to maintain some composure. And I did that fairly successfully until, and it really caught me unawares, I went down to the canteen to get a coffee. I bumped into a junior person within my team. She said some lovely things about the way that the department works and her fidelity to the business. And then she asked me if I was OK.

"It was a moment that caught me. It was somebody else asking me if I was OK. I realised that having thought I was, I actually wasn't. I broke down and apologised to her and excused myself. I went to the toilets, went into a cubicle, locked the door, and just cried. I cried in a way that I hadn't done for probably over ten years.

"I think being human at a time like that is probably the most important thing that you can do."

Heroes and Humans

Not every senior leader is as self-aware as Phil. Many still feel that they have to portray the traditional image of a strong leader, acting as the learned guide to their subordinates and never showing weakness or doubt. Andrew Bryant has been an executive coach for nearly 20 years, working with a variety of senior leaders, and regularly finds that their real issues lie beneath the challenges they bring to him.

Andrew told me, "Some people recognise that they need a coach, sometimes the coach is assigned to them. Often coaching starts with a business challenge: 'I need more executive presence', 'I want more confidence' or 'I want to get to the next level'. As we get into it, we discover that underlying a lot of their success is some insecurity, and suddenly, because they have somebody who acts as a confidant to them that they trust, they open up. My entire professional career I have seen people who on the outside to everybody else are extremely successful, while on the inside are struggling."

Andrew works with volunteer mentors from a Swiss bank for a programme for outreach teenagers in Singapore and the way many of the executives initially act with the teenagers says a lot about their leadership style.

"I coach the mentors to work with the kids and they have to get the kids to open up. But they don't know how to do that. The advice I give them is to be vulnerable.

"I have found that the best thing to do is to be authentic and to tell the kids, 'You know, I struggled, these were my weaknesses and this is what I found worked for me' rather than saying 'this will work for you'. All people need to know is that you're not perfect; you've worked through stuff and there is light at the end of the tunnel. When we are helping people, the key quality is humility, so that if I am helping somebody, often I help myself.

When we are helping people, the key quality is humility, so that if I am helping somebody, often I help myself.

"What blocks help is any kind of air of superiority. These kids open up to me because I don't judge them and that's what I teach the mentors."

Teams look to their leaders to lead but not necessarily to make key decisions in isolation. Great leaders are willing to admit that they don't know the right answers but they take steps to find them. That includes involving their teams in seeking the solution. You look to your leader to make a final decision when the time is right but that doesn't mean that they can't solicit ideas first.

The Power of Failure

In January 2019 a new research paper was published by Harvard Business School arguing how it benefits successful people to be open about their failures[11]. The research team conducted three online experiments and then tested their theory at an event where entrepreneurs competed for investment through pitches.

The premise for the study was that people would be more likely to engage positively with people when they shared their failures as well as successes. Participants scored their reactions to individuals in various scenarios and the team demonstrated that revealing successes and failures led to a decrease in 'malicious envy' (defined as when people wanted a perceived peer to fail) compared to just sharing successes.

I asked study author Professor Alison Wood Brooks and her doctoral advisee, Nicole Abi-Esber how revealing your failures can change the way people perceive you. They told me, "Our pilot study showed that people tend to hide their failures from others as they're happening and speak to very few people about them after they've happened. If we can get over the initial reluctance to reveal failures, there are surprising benefits.

"Doing so decreases malicious envy. It increases benign envy: respect and admiration from others. It also motivates other people to do better themselves. We find suggestive evidence that revealing failures increases the perception of the person sharing as having authentic pride and confidence, and decreases the perception that they are arrogant. So, although it's uncomfortable, it has significant interpersonal benefits."

Revealing failures increases the perception of the person sharing as having authentic pride and confidence, and decreases the perception that they are arrogant.

Professor Brooks and her colleagues found that sharing failure is particularly relevant for managers and leaders; the more senior you are, the greater an impact it's likely to have.

They told me, "For both high-status and medium-status individuals, sharing failures decreased malicious envy, and importantly, did *not* decrease the perceptions of that person's status. It's not just that we envy them less because we think they're lower status and less enviable people, it's that we envy them less specifically because they share failures.

We suspect that the strategy is less relevant for low-status individuals because people don't feel envious of them in the first place.

"Given that we're naturally inclined to share successes, we would recommend taking advantage of these already occurring situations and coupling the sharing of success with sharing failures. For example: during a sales meeting, when somebody shares that they've landed a great client, they can be honest about the unreturned calls and failed pitches they encountered on the path to success. When an author gets a book deal, they can talk about the other publishers that may have rejected them.

"This strategy is especially inspiring for leaders, whose achievements and successes are self-evident but the struggles they overcame to succeed are unobservable unless they share them with their employees."

Where Does a Leader Find the Right Support?

Being willing to be vulnerable is one thing and a change in culture is refreshing. That doesn't mean that the new generation of leaders should throw caution to the wind and tell everyone that they don't know what they are doing!

Whether enlisting the support of an executive coach, a mentor within or outside the business, or a trusted support network, vulnerability needs to be managed effectively. Staff still look to their leaders to lead. They can share questions and challenges with their team but ultimately they still need to inspire confidence that they know what they are doing.

And that's where the role of a trusted sounding board comes in. Just as leading sports stars don't usually ditch their coaches and go it alone when they reach the top, the need for external support can increase as you become more successful. Don't always look to the most obvious people for that support. I find that when I mentor clients I can bring value precisely because I'm not immersed in their business, industry or sector. I'm able to bring a different perspective from the industry-accepted views.

Ivan Misner told me, "Look for an antidote to Group Think. Group Think is a concept that came from the Bay of Pigs with the Kennedy administration, where President Kennedy asked people for their opinion and the only people who spoke up were the people who had Foreign Service experience. He didn't get comments from others and they ended up saying later, 'I thought it was a stupid idea but I didn't think I was the expert.'

"So then, just less than a year later during the Cuban missile crisis, he went around the room and made everyone give their opinion, whether they felt they were qualified or not. He said, 'You don't leave the room until you give me your opinion and you never ever leave the room and say you felt something different and didn't share it'."

You never ever leave the room and say you felt something different and didn't share it.

16.

Being There... as an Organisation

On the evening of 25 January 2008 Geoff McDonald woke with a start, suffering from a massive panic attack. His wife convinced him to go to the doctor who diagnosed anxiety-fuelled depression.

Geoff had been working internationally in a senior role for Unilever for ten years and travelled on a regular basis; it seemed that all the air miles had finally caught up with him.

Since his diagnosis, Geoff has committed much of his time and energy to campaigning and educating people about mental health in the workplace. He told me that there are three commonly accepted triggers that make people more susceptible to depression and anxiety. It can be in your genes, relate to childhood trauma, or what happens to you as an adult.

Geoff explained this to me, "The more that gets thrown at you, the more susceptible you can become to some sort of crucible moment. Financial wellbeing is a big driver. I suppose it was an element of financial concern that was a trigger for me.

"I was travelling all over the world and not sleeping as much as I should because I was on airplanes all the time. When I was back, I was trying to compensate by doing lots of exercise and watching what I was eating and drinking but not taking any time out to recover. It was like I was on this wheel the whole time."

Corporate Responsibility

Excessive travel is not the only source of executive stress. Nick Jonsson, General Manager of EGN Singapore, a community for business leaders, conducted research with members of his network for his book on executive loneliness. Nick found that, from his small sample, 30% of senior executives have experienced a bout of depression and 82% of executives find it difficult to talk about stress and depression in their company.

Nick told me, "The reason that 82% find it difficult to discuss this with their company is that their bosses are often based in another continent. Their teams are spread across Asia and they cannot talk about these issues with the people that they should inspire and motivate.

"The global HR team is often also located on another continent and these topics are not easily brought up over a Skype call. The safest place may be over a casual lunch or after-work drink but the Regional Director based in Singapore does not have this opportunity."

This is just one more example of the types of challenges facing employers, particularly in multinational organisations. Leaders are under increasing pressure to perform but not given an opportunity to relieve that pressure.

Leaders are under increasing pressure to perform but not given an opportunity to relieve that pressure.

One of the major areas Geoff focuses on now is the importance of employers recognising how mental health can affect their staff and creating the right conditions to ensure they feel supported and listened to. I asked him about the culture he encountered in Unilever and it's clear that, like many other companies at the time, it wasn't conducive to picking up issues early and ensuring that any concerns were addressed.

"I don't think there was a recognition of giving time for people to recover, to slow down," Geoff told me. "If we go back to 2008, Unilever was under significant pressure. We had just come through four years of major restructuring. There probably was not much room for recovery and the business was under significant pressure in terms of its performance."

With the higher profile of mental health issues, you would hope that the environment has changed in over ten years since Geoff had his panic attack and diagnosis. I have spoken to people at a number of major organisations where the mental health of staff is high on the agenda and steps are being taken to provide support, such as mental health champions made available for confidential conversations and advice.

While Geoff acknowledges the progress in this area, it's still nowhere near enough for him. "What is good is that we are having the conversation now. Leaders are beginning to recognise the impact that mental ill health is having on the engagement of their employees and on their productivity. We are also beginning to see some leaders telling their stories as a way of getting the conversation going.

"What I have noticed in my work is that four years ago I would talk to business leaders and they would ask me why should we be talking about mental ill health. Today, they are not asking that, they are asking, 'What should we do about this? How should we go about preventing it?'

"But for me that is all still quite reactive. We wait for someone to fall over then we show them all the love and the care that they deserve. Instead why don't we show that a bit earlier so people do not get ill in the first place?"

We wait for someone to fall over then we show them all the love and the care that they deserve. Instead why don't we show that a bit earlier so people do not get ill in the first place?

The shift that Geoff has seen is a step in the right direction but we are probably a long way from the proactive employee care that he wants to see in place. A few months ago, one of my contacts, a senior executive in a well-known professional services firm, complained about wellness programmes and 'snowflake' culture, telling me, "They just need a good night's sleep."

While different industries have taken a lead on creating breakout environments for their staff to enjoy some downtime or put into place policies that limit the hours worked, ultimately most organisations are driven by the bottom line and not everyone truly subscribes to the new culture.

Geoff told me, "I would like senior leaders to become more authentic about the fact that the current environment is psychologically unsafe. Let's invest in resources that will help to maintain or give people a buffer so that they can perform to their best potential.

"In addition, I do not think that senior leaders have fully seen the relationship between health, energy and performance. Because they have not made that connection, when we introduce health initiatives it's in the form of a wellbeing week, we have some bananas next to the till in the canteen, or we say we are going to have no more sweets in our meeting rooms.

"If I introduce a new performance management system, I put a major change programme behind it. With that change programme comes the right level of financial and human resource, influencing of key stakeholders, measuring milestones, celebrating successes, changing some of the processes and systems in the organisation. But when it comes to wellbeing, we just have a week."

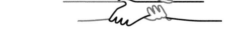

When it comes to wellbeing, we just have a week.

Broadband of Brothers

One company that has impressed me with how seriously they take their responsibility to the people who work there is Hong Kong Broadband Network (HKBN). A fast-growing telecoms provider, the company was founded in 1992 as City Telecom by entrepreneur

Ricky Wong. The business grew rapidly and the culture quickly became one of a workforce equipped to execute effectively their leader's new ideas and instruction.

This meant that a change was needed after Ricky Wong sold the company to a management buyout in 2012. Leaders in the business had excelled at implementing Wong's direction. Now they needed to be able to innovate, guide and lead for themselves.

Co-owner and Head of Talent Engagement and Corporate Social Investment CY Chan was at the forefront of the change. He told me, "We needed to explore new ideas on how to lead this company. We could no longer rely on executors only, we needed leaders who could think, talk about the future and meet the team to make sure the company would do well. We needed to move from a 'leaders and followers' relationship; we needed a lot of new ideas where anyone can be a leader.

"In late 2012 we had a meeting among the management team and decided to use 'Make our Hong Kong a better place to live' as our future core purpose. That decision made a huge difference because today we no longer just focus on making profit. While being profitable, we also want to help Hong Kong people.

"We needed everyone to be on board with the same mission and started to talk about what kind of leadership we required from the management. We focused on two things. One is empowerment and the second one is leading disruption. So, when we evaluate a leader in HKBN we focus on these two things. Empowerment means that you delegate but, at the same time, not just delegate work to your team. You need to develop them.

"You need to make sure that your team deliver the results, not you deliver the results personally. So micro managing no longer works. We want your team members to shine, not you. The more people you develop in the company, the better leader you are. This is how we define empowerment.

We want your team members to shine, not you. The more people you develop in the company, the better leader you are.

"The second is leading disruption. Empowerment is about people; leading disruption is when we evaluate business impact. We focus on what new ideas you have brought to disrupt the way of doing things within your team, the department, the company or even bigger, the market."

Creating a New Culture

This new approach changed the usual flow of help and support. Within HKBN, it's not just a question of teams asking for help from their managers and directors, the leadership will ask for help from their team as well. Within Chinese culture that's a major shift from the norm.

"I think it's down to communication. It's down to expectation. In the Chinese culture it's abnormal to ask for help from other team members, from junior guys or other departments, because it looks like losing face. You're not capable. But in this company we have a culture where asking for help is normal. You have to engage other teams to work together to ensure that we will deliver the results.

"We don't perceive a leader who never makes a mistake as a good leader because this is just telling us that you never try anything. We also like to know what kind of mistakes and how many you have learned from.

We don't perceive a leader who never makes a mistake as a good leader because this is just telling us that you never try anything.

"We do that because, as a good leader, you should have new ideas and new ideas will never be 100% right."

Asking for help or admitting failure has become the culture of the company. HKBN encourage their partners and team members to innovate and try new things and learning from mistakes is a key part of that. Leaders are expected to create the culture that allows their team to be courageous and shine, not to be the font of all knowledge.

Co-ownership

I often talk about how often I see competition within a company rather than collaboration. Employers view team and individual targets as the best incentive for high performance but can miss the damage such an approach can do to the company's culture.

Surely it's better to ensure that everyone is invested in the success of the organisation as a whole rather than just their own area of responsibility. Team or individual incentives lead to siloed thinking and a lack of support across teams and departments. The ownership structure of HKBN acts instead to encourage a mutually supportive culture.

Team or individual incentives lead to siloed thinking and a lack of support across teams and departments.

After the management buyout, 100 senior managers were invited to take a stake in the company and become co-owners. Ninety of them took up the offer. CY attributes much of the transparency and willingness to ask for help to this co-ownership structure.

"The management team is no longer the top six guys. It is the hundreds of co-owners including the additional new co-owners after our IPO (Initial Public Offering) in 2015. We share everything to do with the business within this group. It then cascades down because, as co-owners, to make sure that the company succeeds, we need to make sure that everyone understands the direction. From the top all the way down to team members. It needs to be much more transparent than before.

"We want everyone to understand and work together to make sure that we achieve our goals. I think that is the core reason why we have become much more transparent in this process."

Organisations don't need a co-operative model to learn from the benefits of this approach. Shifting to team goals and understanding how each part of an organisation feeds the success of the whole can drive a similar outcome. While competition has its place internally, I would argue that collaboration should take centre stage and incentive programmes as well as other forms of recognition should reflect this.

If that happens then it will be much more likely that people will feel free to speak up because it's in all of their colleagues' interests to support them. That doesn't mean that you shouldn't encourage and reward individual success though, as we're about to discover.

17.

GREAT TEAMS ARE MADE UP OF GREAT INDIVIDUALS

Successful teams all thrive on openness and vulnerability. As we explored in the last chapter, the 'All for One and One for All' spirit can be the difference between a group of great individuals working for themselves and failing to reach their potential together and a team achieving massive success.

Sir Clive Woodward has enjoyed success in both business and sport. He's well known for coaching the England rugby team to World Cup glory and going on to be Director of Football for Southampton FC and Director of Sport at the British Olympic Association. He also has a track record in business, building up and selling a successful computer leasing company and today he runs a thriving consultancy and technology business.

Sir Clive told me, "Sport is a business but sometimes I think the business world puts too much emphasis on teamwork. If there is a great secret to running teams, the key ingredient is to get every individual really enjoying what they are doing, really trying to improve themselves. If you get every individual working hard trying to make themselves better and you're helping them, the team stuff becomes quite straightforward."

If you get every individual working hard trying to make themselves better and you're helping them, the team stuff becomes quite straightforward.

Woodward told me how he introduced a buddy system into his squads, pairing players with each other and making sure that they each had the other's back when required. Such a system would be integral to ensuring that people felt able to share with each other.

"There's that fine balance between what is affecting your performance and what isn't, hence the buddy system. You may not want to discuss it with me, your boss, but you may discuss it with a colleague at the same level as you, especially if you know that person well. Then you make a joint decision.

"I like any player or athlete that I am working with to know me well, but it is also important to me for them to know that they have a support system within the team of people that they are actually working with."

All that Glitters is not Golden

The 2018 football World Cup saw a surprising resurgence by the England team, who reached the semi-finals of the tournament against even the most optimistic expectations. The surprise was even greater because this was a team with no superstars, in stark contrast to the so-called 'Golden Generation' that preceded it. That team, featuring world-class footballers such as David Beckham, Frank Lampard, John Terry and Steven Gerrard, had failed to produce anything close to the riches supporters and the media felt their talents deserved.

Perhaps one of the biggest differences between the achievements of the two sides lay in their ability to open up to each other. Centre-back Rio Ferdinand, a mainstay of the 'Golden Generation', told *The Times* newspaper that everyone's dream team were never likely to succeed because of a lack of trust[12].

"It overshadowed things. It killed that England team, that generation. One year we would have been fighting Liverpool to win the League; another year it would be Chelsea. I was never going to walk into the England dressing room and open up to Frank Lampard, Ashley Cole, John Terry or Joe Cole at Chelsea, or Steven Gerrard or Jamie Carragher at Liverpool.

"I wouldn't open up because of the fear they would take something back to their club and use it against us, to make them better than us. I didn't really want to engage with them. I was so engrossed, so obsessed with winning with Manchester United – nothing else mattered."

By contrast, the 2018 squad were encouraged to talk to each other and share. Sports psychologist Dr Pippa Grange was appointed Head of People and Team Development at the Football Association in November 2018 and focused on making the players less inhibited.

According to reports, Grange's work included getting the players to sit down together in small groups to share their life experiences and anxieties, and to reveal intimate truths about their character and what drives them. The point, according to Head Coach Gareth Southgate, is to build trust, 'making them closer, with a better understanding of each other'[13].

Grange's work included getting the players to sit down together in small groups to share their life experiences and anxieties, and to reveal intimate truths about their character and what drives them.

According to Sir Clive Woodward, "Like all things in sport, there is no right or wrong way of doing this. I was probably somewhere in the middle of the two approaches. The thing about the England rugby team, just because you have had success and you end up winning a World Cup, everyone assumes that it's all hunky-dory but this doesn't just happen. We worked hard to bring unity to our team and it wasn't always easy.

"The England rugby team was probably very similar to the England football team in many ways because you have players coming from rival clubs. Take Leicester and Northampton, there's a huge history there. I would say categorically some of the players from Northampton didn't get on with the players from Leicester and vice versa. So how do you handle that?"

One of Woodward's favourite approaches was to use the buddy system discussed earlier. Woodward consciously buddied up players from rival clubs or people who he knew didn't even like each other.

"The buddy system was basically 'You are going to look after your buddy 24/7 365'. I changed it about once a month, so I would move people around and I would start off by saying 'I want you to look after your buddy in terms of making sure that if you are going to be late for a meeting you have got someone to ring. If there is something going on, you have got this person'.

"But it was most important on the field of play, when it's all kicking off.

"The players got that because I led it very much from a playing side. If your buddy is injured, if your teammate gets into a scrap, if he gets into a conflict with the referee, you must go up and help him. It's not just the next person, your buddy goes and helps you."

One intriguing innovation was wristbands that the players wore during the matches bearing key messages they had agreed beforehand and needed to remember. The twist, however, was that players wore wristbands with the messages that their buddy needed to recall, not their own.

"So, you go to him and remind him. If he is tired, fatigued, injured, you remind him of the key three or four points. Subliminally what actually happened was they started to get to know each other better."

Battle Buddies

Sir Clive's buddy system isn't just to be found in the world of sport; in the military those close-knit relationships are absolutely key. You might not be willing to share with your team as a whole but you need a 'battle buddy' to be there for you.

I asked former New Zealand marine Dion Jensen, a veteran of the Balkans War and close protection duties in Iraq, just how easy it is to share in the military. It turns out that it's not straightforward, and while there may be good reasons for that, perhaps that's one explanation why so many veterans suffer with PTSD.

Dion told me, "When I was struggling, I went to a civilian mate to show my vulnerability because I wasn't going to show it to my military crew. That was easy and he knows me very well. Not everyone has that network outside the army and that's where a lot of problems occur.

"In the military, yes, you have a battle buddy. On every team you are closer to one person than you are to everybody else. It could be your fire team; in the sniper team it's your spotter; in the gun group, that's your number two. Over in Iraq I had a guy called GT. I would go and sit with him and cry if I had to. I could do that without shame because we were battle buddies.

"The reason why you don't want to appear weak to your team is that you don't want them to lose trust in your abilities, because that's your value to the team. If we're about to go into something and they look over and they see me, they know that I'm going to stay with them 100%. I'm rock solid and I'll die for them. That's it.

The reason why you don't want to appear weak to your team is that you don't want them to lose trust in your abilities, because that's your value to the team.

"I'm scared that if I say that I'm struggling with this stuff, they're going to look over and say 'I can't rely on this guy, I can't trust him'."

Dion's experience suggests that there are very few outlets for help and support within the armed forces. And with constantly high levels of stress, fear and trauma, that can only lead to problems.

"As soon as you say you are struggling with something you get rubber-stamped that you cannot deploy and that's going to affect both your promotional status and your deployment status. Your greatest value is deploying with your team, and as soon as you ask for help the first thing that happens is you are no longer able to do so.

"You are removed from your family."

18.

How Can Organisations and Leaders Encourage Vulnerability and Sharing?

The renowned football manager Pep Guardiola tells a story from his time as Manager of Catalan giants FC Barcelona.

Barcelona reached the Champions League final, the pinnacle of European club football, in 2009. But Guardiola faced a selection crisis with first choice full-backs Dani Alves and Éric Abidal both unavailable.

Guardiola's solution was to select Malian midfielder Seydou Keita out of position. Guardiola explains that his plans were turned on their head when Keita approached him and told him, "Do not pick me. There are better options than me at right back." Keita knew that this conversation could mean that he would not even be in the squad, although he was named as a substitute. He sacrificed his role because he said, "The team would suffer if I was put there."

This story was shared with me by Professor Damian Hughes, author of *The Barcelona Way*[14], a book where he combines his passion for sport with a model of different business cultures. Damian told me, "Guardiola uses that as a gold-plated standard to say that this guy was prepared to sacrifice his own moment of glory. He could have kept quiet and played."

In his book, Damian outlines Guardiola's approach as the classic example of a 'Commitment Culture', an approach to team development that puts people at its heart and which, according to Damian, is far more successful than any alternative approach.

Damian explained to me, "The research suggests that if you do not harness the power of a culture, there will be five different types that will emerge almost organically.

"The first one is Star Culture where you go out of your way to bring in the most talented people. You often pay them the highest salaries, give them the best resources and then hope they will come together and the cumulative effect of what they are capable of will be greater than the sum of its parts.

"Former Real Madrid Head Coach Julen Lopetegui told me that 'in a culture like this, everyone is head waiter but nobody wants to wash the dishes'. Real Madrid, with their 'Galacticos' recruitment strategy of buying the world's best players, was a classic example of Star Culture. A lack of vulnerability was a key characteristic of that team.

"The second type of culture is an Autocracy. In the business world you may have a charismatic founder where it tends to be their way or the highway. You think of somewhere like Apple under Steve Jobs, especially in his first incarnation; when he was removed, the vacuum created by his absence was huge.

"The third type is a Bureaucracy, where middle managers contain most of the power, centred around rules, regulations and procedures. Decisions have to be made by a committee; everything moves at a glacial pace.

"The fourth type of culture is an Engineering Culture, where technical skills are prized above anything else. You recruit people for having a deep knowledge in a specific technical area.

"Research suggests that Commitment Culture is around 22% more successful than any of those other types. There is also evidence that says people will stay loyal to a Commitment Culture even when they are offered a pay raise up to 36% to go elsewhere.

"Commitment Culture creates organisations that have a clear sense of purpose, a clear set of identified behaviours and values that define the organisation and put people at the centre of it.

Commitment Culture creates organisations that have a really clear sense of purpose, a clear set of identified behaviours and values that define the organisation and put people at the centre of it.

"Ten years ago Barcelona adopted that principle. Their performance had fallen off a cliff and then, rather than hire and fire in the style common across European football, they decided to use culture as a competitive advantage. They put in place a whole series of initiatives to develop these high levels of trust that are almost endemic within Commitment Cultures."

Damian explained there are three trademark behaviours that are central to a Commitment Culture. Behaviours that are non-negotiable. "We are not talking about values," Damian explained, "because people can state adherence to a value without ever having to demonstrate it."

Txiki Begiristain, the Director of Football at Barcelona, told Damian, "Your talent will get you as far as our dressing room door, your behaviour decides if we will keep you within that dressing room."

Damian told me, "The first behaviour is humility. Begiristain told me that by the time a player gets as far as the dressing room door there is a high chance they are going to be a highly fêted, richly rewarded person. The club made clear to them 'We have no desire for you to come into this environment and show off your status symbols of wealth and success.'

"They argued that such behaviour would indicate a lack of humility and a lack of the ability to listen and learn. If you cannot listen and learn, you cannot improve and contribute to the organisation. They reinforced this by telling players that they were not allowed to drive anything other than a club car to training, it didn't matter how expensive their sports car was.

"The second behaviour was hard work. It took hard work to be considered for the Barcelona first team but they wanted to reinforce that this was just the beginning. You continue to invest in your talent and work hard, not come in and just coast along. You come and train, try new things and learn.

"The third behaviour was putting the team above self-interest. If there is ever a clash between what is right for you as an individual and what might be right for your teammate, choose the teammate option.

"The true evidence of a culture is how people behave when no one is watching. Whenever Barcelona had a close chance to score, Guardiola's assistant would watch the reaction of the players on the bench, who had not been selected. If there were players that did not jump up in response to the near miss, he made a note of that and then they would address it with the player directly."

The Personal Touch

Colin Wright, a former Senior Vice President at both MasterCard and Global Payments, shared his belief that the focus for any business should be on the individual first and the rest will follow.

Colin told me, "At MasterCard, as Head of Global Sales Development, there were a number of challenges associated with selecting a set of corporate standards and practices that had to be introduced in salesforces around the world. What resonates with employees in one country or region does not necessarily resonate within another.

"The idea that one size fits all is a bit of a 'rabbit hole'. If you are coming across in a way that fails to account for nuances of each individual, you may come across as a rigid manager. The importance of this point is further magnified when determining how best to manage and lead unique and possibly conflicting personalities (or teams), country to country and region by region.

"I always go back to what resonates most with me and others around me. The answer lies in sincerity, caring and a genuine approach to business, employee by employee. It is also about being present in the moment and identifying the unique characteristics, dimensions and requirements of each individual – it is not about force-fitting unique employees into broad corporate categories or profiles."

The answer lies in sincerity, caring and a genuine approach to business, employee by employee.

Changes to modern working styles and environments have perhaps created more opportunities for businesses to respond to individual needs and challenges, making people feel more comfortable opening up to their colleagues and bosses.

Michelle Settecase, who does most of her work for global consultancy firm Ernst and Young (EY) from her home in Ohio, has seen the benefits of this. She told me, "I regularly talk to people who work from home and have dogs barking or children playing in the background or they are in a café somewhere. This has made it easier to connect personally with people because it is not a formal phone call.

"What I find most interesting is that I work with a virtual team of men and women around the globe, nobody is sitting next to each other. I cannot reach out and grab my teammates. That makes it more of a challenge to be vulnerable; I am not personally across the table. When you cannot reach out and grab somebody's hand, you need to build in chat time, build in personal development time. Use video conferencing. Not everything can be written word.

"Just connect. Sometimes you have to schedule the time but you do not have to have a meeting. Just ask, 'What did you do this weekend? How is it going? What is going on?'

"I find that as a team lead and as someone who wants to champion being authentic, if you do not speak up and say something then nobody else will. That takes a lot of courage. It is harder to be vulnerable though when you have people around you who will not let you. Or perceive being vulnerable as being weak."

Launched in 2019, the Inside Out campaign is leading the way in the UK to address this challenge and encourage people to feel comfortable speaking out and opening up, particularly in the field of mental health.

Inside Out have created a 'Leaderboard' of business leaders in well-known organisations, including HSBC, Tesco and Goldman Sachs, who have shared their challenges with mental health in the hope of creating a ripple effect, normalising such conversations across their organisations and beyond.

Planning For and Learning From Mistakes

We've already looked at the importance of creating a culture where mistakes are embraced as an opportunity rather than punished. A culture where being vulnerable is seen as a weakness would not sit well with Sir Clive Woodward. Part of the culture that Sir Clive tries to instil in any organisation with which he works, sporting or business, is that mistakes are expected.

"I'll say to any business, any team that I work with, 'My goal is to go from here to here but I've never had a team that has gone in a straight line. It's always all over the place. You have big wins, big losses, big setbacks and you have got to handle each in equal measure.'

"You have got to know how to handle winning, you have got to know how to handle losing and you have got to know how to handle setbacks. The key thing to me is that I probably discuss losing more than any other coach.

You have got to know how to handle winning, you have got to know how to handle losing and you have got to know how to handle setbacks.

"If you lose a big deal there is no point afterwards asking 'What the hell do we do now?'. You have got to discuss winning and losing up front. That way, if you do lose the match or the big deal, everyone knows how to handle it."

The type of vulnerability and honesty that Seydou Keita showed at Barcelona, part of the Commitment Culture that puts team needs above individual reward, is key to the open conversations that Sir Clive wants to see.

A Safe Space

Often, it's the corporate culture that prevents people from sharing. This is something that Andrew Grill recognised during his time in senior roles at organisations such as IBM, Telstra and British Aerospace.

Andrew told me, "I have been in large organisations where things get done through politics, so you can't show any weakness because that then puts you on the back foot. I don't think that will change until we have a generational shift where the people who are not programmed and trained how to handle this are retired."

As previously discussed, companies are increasingly taking positive steps forward to change their environment and make it easier for people to share. One of my major concerns is that these initiatives are often volunteer-led and don't always get real support from senior management. Top executives may pay lip-service but that doesn't always translate into real leadership. I'm aware of volunteers who have had to give up their role because of resentment from their team and line managers.

It also spoke volumes that one large bank whose staff do a lot of great work in this space would not allow the same staff to talk about their efforts and ideas for this book. Their communications team told them not to participate in interviews or mention the organisation's name. In an industry beset by bad press, it amazes me that they would be so distrustful of an opportunity to do something positive and demonstrates a lack of real leadership in this area.

As discussed in chapter 13, strong robust mentoring programmes that allow mentees to select mentors and peers who fit their desired criteria do exist but we need to see more of them, together with more training on effective mentoring. To make that safe space even more secure, cross-company schemes where mentees can work with executives from other firms can work well to encourage people to truly open up.

As positive as they can be, we don't always need formal arrangements or named volunteers to encourage people to open up. It's great to have such programmes but the onus should be on all organisations to create a culture where people feel happy to share with their colleagues and managers and where staff encourage each other to open up.

19.

Do We Allow Our Politicians to Get Things Wrong?

"When we got on Air Force One the last time, I cried for about thirty minutes. It was just the release of eight years of feeling like we had to do everything perfectly. That there wasn't a margin of error. That we couldn't make mistakes. That we couldn't slip. That our tone had to be perfect." **Michelle Obama**[15]

"To those waiting with bated breath for that favourite media catchphrase, the U-turn, I have only one thing to say: You turn if you want to. The lady's not for turning!" **Margaret Thatcher**[16]

If we are going to encourage more people to share, own up to mistakes and admit that they don't have the solutions to the challenges that face them, we need to ensure that we create the right environment. And lead from the top.

Politics has been portrayed for too long as them against us; the landed classes subjugating the working poor; big business winning at the expense of the unemployed; Red versus Blue. There's no room for nuance, particularly in systems where third parties and independent candidates historically have been squeezed out.

The media has perpetuated these divisions, driving politicians like Margaret Thatcher to make statements such as "The lady's not for turning". Positioning self-belief and conviction in your own truth as a strength, while at the same time leaving no room for flexibility, acceptance of mistakes or willingness to learn.

A media, now supercharged by social sites like Twitter, swells the ranks of commentators by millions and magnifies every slip, every doubt and every marginal turn.

A media, now supercharged by social sites like Twitter, swells the ranks of commentators by millions and magnifies every slip, every doubt and every marginal turn.

These problems became magnified in the UK in the last few years, with the debate over Brexit becoming increasingly rancorous both in Parliament and in the country as a whole, and the trend continuing with rows over lockdowns and masks. Positions became more entrenched, with people far less likely to listen to other arguments.

For James Cleverly, former Chairman of the Conservative Party and a UK Government Minister, there is in politics a 'massive disincentive to show any kind of vulnerability or any kind of weakness, or any lack of knowledge'.

James explained, "I have worked in a number of different environments. I've been through the military, I've been through small and big business. In those environments there is an understanding that making mistakes is part of a learning and evolutionary process.

"In politics, particularly at Westminster where you've got that real, obsessive gaze, there is a massive disincentive to act in a way that would be normal in any other walk of life. I think some of that is around the very immediate, confrontational nature of how we work. If you make even a modest course correction on a policy, the response is 'It's a U-turn, it's a climbdown'."

James believes that many of the run of the mill accusations across the political divide are artificial and manageable. However, there are times when the pressure brought by the combination of the public spotlight and the adversarial nature of politics means that jobs are far less secure and people are sacrificed far too easily.

"You are under genuine pressure and obviously we have had ministers who have had to resign. When you have got that kind of baying, it's almost a mob mindset that, I can imagine, is really difficult."

James' Conservative Party was at the centre of a high-profile, while loudly denied, policy U-turn which derailed the launch of their manifesto at the beginning of the 2017 General Election.

A Conservative pledge to bring down the cost of caring for people in their own homes by making them pay more of the costs themselves was branded a 'dementia tax' and led to a drop in support at the polls[17]. The Prime Minister subsequently announced plans for a cap on costs but denied a U-turn and the policy itself was quietly shelved.

"That's a classic example," James told me. "I think it's a good example because it shows how mistakes are made. Typically, the difference between a good and a bad decision is small and often there are a number of points where an intervention could or should have happened that didn't. A bad decision and a good decision start at the same place and there will always be opportunities for people to intervene and stop it going wrong."

Stop Keeping Your Counsel

James went through the mistakes made in the development of the social care policy with me point by point, and I asked him why people didn't take any of those opportunities to step in and whether there is a culture in politics where people are afraid to speak up. There is a danger that this is not something that is unique to politics but which plagues business, industry and our personal lives as well.

"In that instance, I think that the unwillingness to press the stop button was particularly acute because we were in the middle of a snap election, so everything was happening very quickly.

"If you are about to launch a manifesto and you get a sniff of something that you feel a bit unsure of and you say 'I want to stop the whole process because there is something which doesn't feel right to me', then people will say 'Well, if you are going to do that you had better turn it around within the hour, not days, because that is hitting the printers on Wednesday.'

"It's not integrity, it's self-confidence, because the question you are then forced to ask yourself is 'Is this really a problem? Is it of the scale that I think it might be? Even if it is a problem, is delaying every other thing that is going into that manifesto worth it?'

"It is important that there is always a mechanism where you can intervene and do something to stop the process. It doesn't mean to say that everyone gets a veto on everything, because then government would just grind to a halt."

One of the other issues that stood out for me in James' description of the shortfalls of the social care policy is the vacuum in which it was designed. James explained, "When the policy was being developed it was in a vacuum. There was a small number of people working on it and, as is often the case with a small team, you get some very effective work but you get a distillation of the idea. So, everyone agrees with everyone, who then agrees with everyone, who agrees with everyone.

"It's really easy to get to a point where no one has unplugged themselves from the matrix and just seen what is going on in the world, just to double check. Everyone's got their sleeves rolled up, everyone is stuck in.

Everyone agrees with everyone, who then agrees with everyone, who agrees with everyone. It's really easy to get to a point where no one has unplugged themselves from the matrix.

"What they didn't do is that periodic sanity check. They got right to the end of the process, the manifesto was developed quickly and they didn't have the group discussion dissemination process you would normally expect."

Surely this is another symptom of our binary politics, the unreasonable expectations that we put on to our politicians, the expectation that they have all the answers. James agrees.

It was refreshing to have a brief insight into a more vulnerable and less self-assured Government in the early days of the Covid-19 induced lockdown in the spring of 2020. Health Secretary Matt Hancock responded to people who disagreed with the Government's approach by inviting disagreement.

Hancock told the BBC's Andrew Marr, "I welcome the debate. I don't mind having a debate about it; I listen and I try to find out if there's something that we haven't thought of, something we need to consider. Because all that matters is getting this response right[18]."

I don't mind having a debate about it; I listen and I try to find out if there's something that we haven't thought of, something we need to consider.

This, for me, represents a much more mature and effective approach to political decision-making but stands out primarily because it seems to be so rare. But what happens away from the photographers' lens?

Friends in Different Corners

Despite the adversarial nature of politics, highlighted by the former British Labour Shadow Chancellor of the Exchequer claiming that he can't be a friend with Conservative MPs[19] and the insults thrown by Republican Congressman Ted Yoho at his Democrat opponent Alexandria Ocasio-Cortez on the steps of the

US Capitol[20], support on an individual level can still come from the most unlikely places.

Former Leader of the Liberal Democrats, Jo Swinson, remembers early in her career when support came from an unexpected quarter. When she was about to face her first Ministerial Questions in the House of Commons, former Conservative Minister Sir Michael Fallon reassured her.

In her book *Equal Power*[21] Jo wrote: 'From unlikely quarters, the reassurance did come, though. Michael Fallon was also a new minister but had previously served as a minister in the 1990s – an archetypal Conservative who I didn't expect to bond with. Seeing that I looked rather nervous, he quietly confided that he was too. "But you've done this before!" I said. He replied that it was 20 years ago, and anyway, the fear never goes away and nor should it.

'We all have this power at our disposal, to see when others – even our competitors or opponents – are approaching a difficult challenge and an extra boost will help; at the right moment it might be as little as a smile or a kind word at that human level that can make all the difference.'

"There is a lot of camaraderie in the House of Commons," Jo explained to me. "I particularly notice it among women and think that is because there is a recognition of shared vulnerability. We both know some of the sexist rubbish we have to put up with and so you've got that bond before you even open your mouth.

"The other thing that's interesting about that story of support from Michael Fallon is that I don't I think I would have had that help if it hadn't been clear that I was finding it a little bit scary. I think showing vulnerability gives the other person permission to not be seen as patronising or as overstepping the normal boundaries but to take it out of an adversarial level to a normal level.

I think showing that vulnerability gives the other person the permission to not be seen as patronising or as overstepping the normal boundaries.

"I think that human connection is quite important in work, whatever your line of work is. Whether it's somebody working for a competing business, or working in another part of the organisation where there are some tensions, actually remember that shared humanity, shared goals, what you've got in common. As Jo Cox[22] famously said in her maiden speech 'We've got more in common than that which divides us' and I think that is so true."

James Cleverly believes that while robust debate and criticism of the opposition are a core and legitimate part of British politics, it is important to maintain positive relationships with parliamentary adversaries.

"I've been criticised by people on the opposition benches and vice versa, and it's a funny one because in order to continue a successful working relationship in this place, you have to be able to rub shoulders and work on committees or party parliamentary groups. To make that work, you have to maintain a good personal relationship with people you have publicly and regularly been very critical of.

"As an outsider looking in, it means that the criticism can look synthetic, or that it's just a bit of a game. It's the nature of our system but, by the same token, you have to separate the personal from the professional."

Building trusted relationships with people who have opposing viewpoints can help us to move out of the echo chamber that we hear so much about. Social media has exacerbated the extent to which we seek reinforcement of our own views rather than challenging the way we think to make sure we're on the right track.

Coping Mechanisms

How do leading politicians cope with the potentially toxic nature of the system they operate within? What can they do to deal with the attacks from their opposite numbers, from the media and from the public, particularly on social media?

As a minister, Jo Swinson found resilience to be a core part of her role, a resilience that she needed in spades when she lost her seat as Leader of the Party in the 2019 General Election.

When Jo was elected as Lib Dem leader, she came under sustained attack from supporters of the Labour Party for her record while in government but it's something she had already become used to.

"In politics, particularly when I was a Government Minister in the coalition, it was significant. Of course, you are constantly questioning yourself, trying to work out what the right thing to do is. How do you do that within the constraints of trying to compromise with a coalition partner that has quite different principles from your own? There is no magic answer.

"There's that sort of easy purity of opposition, but when you're actually faced with trying to make decisions, you realise things are so much more complicated and there is no obvious solution. You do the best you can and you will make mistakes because we are all human. It's hard to admit those mistakes because the penalty is being pilloried in the public eye. We don't make it easy for people to admit that they got something wrong in their political life. That's not healthy."

We don't make it easy for people to admit that they got something wrong in their political life. That's not healthy.

Jo regrets not following her instincts when it came to the controversial tuition fees policy that has haunted the Liberal Democrats since their days in coalition. Having campaigned to abolish university tuition fees, they were then junior partners in a coalition government that actually increased them.

"I recognise from a Liberal Democrat perspective that tuition fees was an obvious one where we did a lot to try to improve the policy but we entirely messed up the politics. My instincts at the time were 'We can't possibly do this' and I think if we had more experience in government, we would have dealt with it differently. We saw constraints that were there that we could have challenged but we were to a degree naïve because none of us had been in government before. Two years later we would have understood what you can't do anything about and vice versa.

"Sometimes you make a change like that and you can do it without a very public mea culpa; sometimes you have to put your hands up. Part of the key to that is authenticity. One of the things I've done when making difficult decisions in my political life is written a blog, a few hundred words, about why I've come to that decision. Whether that was going into the coalition in the first place, whether it's tuition fees, or how I voted on issues like Syria; controversial issues where people take different views.

"I've found just being quite transparent about what my thought process has been has taken a lot of the sting out of it."

I've found just being quite transparent about what my thought process has been has taken a lot of the sting out of it.

A Less Toxic Politics

Despite its adversarial environment, there clearly is some hope in politics. But we need to see more examples of shared humanity and less intransigence.

James Cleverly believes that there are moments of positivity that can be built upon. Going back to the core point, there are a number of occasions where all of us, collectively, rise above the environment we create.

"Prime Minister's Questions are very raw because it's confrontational. And yet if someone has come back from ill health for example, the chamber will fall silent, and when they come to the end of their question, you will hear a very calm 'yeeer' which is our way of saying 'Despite everything you are one of us.'

"It's these little moments. They are often subtle, sometimes too subtle to be noticed by the outside world; but to the individual in question it makes a big difference. Support is often offered quite freely. The interesting point is it's rarely solicited. I don't know whether that's just how it's always going to be, whether we will evolve.

"Maybe we are just taking everything here slower and maybe we will get there. But at the moment, despite lots of evidence that there are people willing to be supportive, we are really, really bad at asking for help."

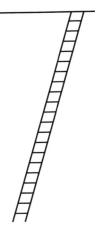

SECTION FIVE
HOW DO WE DIFFER?

20.

How Do Women and Men Differ in Our Willingness to Seek Help?

Although we have seen the growth of the 'metrosexual' male over recent years, with lots of talk of the 21st century man being more in touch with his feelings, the impression I got from many conversations on the topic is that women are still perceived as more likely to share their challenges.

Jo Swinson told me, "Women are encouraged to talk more from an early age and there's a lot of evidence that suggests, when it comes to talking about feelings and emotions, the vocabulary is more developed in girls early on.

"It is often a lot harder for men. The downside can be that men bottle things up and don't deal with them. Men can feel they are fighting on their own; in some cases that can have very significant effects on mental health.

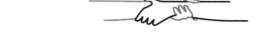

Men can feel they are fighting on their own; in some cases that can have very significant effects on mental health.

"This is a gender role problem in society that we need to be aware of and make sure that men get support when they are struggling and it's not seen as unmanly to talk about things when they get on top of you."

One person trying to provide that support is Luke Ambler. After his 23-year-old brother-in-law took his own life, Luke quit his successful Rugby League career to create an outlet for young men who otherwise pursue a similar route. Luke was a Super League regular and Ireland international with a World Cup on the horizon but his brother-in-law's death hit hard and the need to make a difference was more compelling.

Luke's solution was to set up 'ANDYSMANCLUB', named in memory of his brother-in-law. The network of groups has grown rapidly and he sees hundreds of men come to regular meetings to share.

Men go along to ANDYSMANCLUB for a range of reasons, the motivation isn't important. The key is that they have somewhere they can feel comfortable sharing.

Luke told me, "There is depression, there is anxiety, there are people who have broken up with their partner, people who want to come out as gay, people in debt, gamblers, alcoholics, drug addicts, domestic violence victims, the list could go on. If someone comes, we just say we are all going through storms, let's help each other through."

Luke's experience suggests that while gender expectations may stop men from sharing when they first attend, as they get to know the other people in the room the level of engagement shifts.

"Generally, on their first time in the room, visitors will look at each other's feet. It can take a couple of sessions to look into anyone's eyes, then they sit up, shoulders back, chests out and start to come into themselves and feel that it's a safe space.

"When they come through that door and start to listen to other people, they realise that they are not alone. When you go into a room with 40 or 50 other men and you are sitting next to a bloke on one side who has been through a similar situation to you, you realise 'actually I'm not weird, I'm not weak, I don't need to be embarrassed, I'm not a burden'.

When they come through that door and start to listen to other people, they realise that they are not alone.

"Then they can start to open up and I think that's a big changing point."

Gender Roles

Senior Indian businesswoman Sarika Bhattacharyya believes that gender roles in India impact how people share. "The largest part of the population in India still live in small towns and rural areas. Many are illiterate as well as uneducated and in quite a few places, even where there is an educated population, women are still seen as inferior.

"In that kind of situation, vulnerability becomes a positive virtue for a woman. If I am vulnerable and innocent, I will be seen as the best person for an Indian man to take home and get married. But I if I am seen as a strong, independent woman in the workplace who is questioning people, then I am trying to fit into the trousers and shoes of a man, which is not acceptable."

Despite cultural expectations specific to gender roles, there are some cases where, rather than being a male or female issue, the challenge lies more in masculine and feminine traits. Particularly toxic is the alpha male stereotype, where the man is expected to be dominant and strong and communicate that strength in a purely masculine, insensitive way.

Despite cultural expectations specific to gender roles, there are some cases where, rather than being a male or female issue, the challenge lies more in masculine and feminine traits.

As someone who transitioned from being perceived as a 'butch' gay woman to a relatively effeminate man, Robbie Samuels has found that expectations of him tend to revolve as much around those personality traits as his gender.

"I think people perceive whatever they see in me as not alpha male. I never aspired to be an alpha man. Because I started out as a trans man I feel free to be much more expressive about how I am in the world. If there's a pinnacle of masculinity, I'm not going to achieve it.

"I really resisted the idea that I was going to make this physical transition and then suddenly be stereotypically male, so I think that I compensated by being more vulnerable in spaces, by sharing more, by stepping back."

Women in the Workplace

Society's expectations of women's vulnerability don't seem to have found their way into the world of work, at least not if you are a woman who wants to make a real impression and carve out a successful career. I've often noted how many of the female business role models in the media tend to portray more masculine than feminine traits.

Vanessa Vallely, Founder of WearetheCity.com, a website for professional women, told me, "If you are in an industry or in a division where it's quite alpha or male-dominated, then you might have a tendency to adopt those behaviours because you would feel as if you need to be the brand of the company in order to survive.

"I went through that, wearing pinstriped suits and making decisions that didn't play to my strengths as a woman. I was hiding some of the emotional intelligence that I had, my attitude towards risk, and looking at the collective attitude, thinking that is what I need to adopt."

Vanessa told me that a toxic masculine culture in the workplace prevents women being themselves and opening up, leading to a culture that damages the potential for progress for the individual and the organisation as a whole.

"An alpha male environment doesn't drive being authentic. If you are feeling emotional or upset about something, you wouldn't feel you could share it in that kind of environment. Allowing yourself to be vulnerable is very team dependent. If you have seen that kind of behaviour exhibited, it's OK.

Allowing yourself to be vulnerable is very team dependent. If you have seen that kind of behaviour exhibited, it's OK.

"We are in a world of innovation and disruption. Back in my day it wasn't OK to make mistakes, there was finger pointing. Unless we make mistakes, we will never innovate and we won't build the culture in organisations or the products and services we want to see in the future.

"Unless you are in a culture that encourages you to be authentic and share, you are just going to suppress it. The women that I have spoken to tell me that ongoing suppression leads to resentment because you can't bring your true self to work and the benefit we bring to organisations is that diversity of people turning up as their true selves."

Apurva Purohit, one of India's most influential media leaders, has had similar experiences. She is very clear that vulnerability for women in the workplace is not an option. "If you are a professional woman, asking for help or showing any kind of vulnerability is seen as a weakness. Women are still fighting a battle to be acknowledged as good leaders.

"There are very clear stereotypes in operation. When you are trying to be taken seriously as a woman leader, you end up being harsher and tougher than you naturally would. Showing a single sign of vulnerability, which could be either asking for help or showing some emotion, is seen as over the top.

When you are trying to be taken seriously as a woman leader, you end up being harsher and tougher than you naturally would.

"The stereotypes women are fighting are immense. One is the struggle to be seen as a working person, a person with a corporate entity in her own right. Women are also struggling with the need to win the respect of our male colleagues.

"For example, if I am on a board and talking, I get talked over a lot. The other male board members do not hesitate to interrupt me. They do not hesitate to take what I am saying and craft it in their own words in a more aggressive manner. They do 'mansplaining' with me a lot. Because they are doing this so much, I have to work hard to ensure there is no tentativeness in my approach.

"I have to prepare diligently for board meetings, both in terms of reading up on what has been sent out in advance but also mentally getting ready. I prepare myself to use strong words and short sentences. That is how you should speak. Do not say 'maybe'.

"If this is the context I am operating in, asking questions is just not acceptable. I recognise that maybe if I ask three questions, I will get more clarity and therefore my solution will be that much better."

A Changing Landscape

One common theme throughout many of my conversations on this topic, as with others in this book, is that the world is changing and younger generations have different expectations. Apurva pointed out that, "The next generation is coming into the workforce with the clear intention that they want both career and family. They also see far more women than we saw, as their bosses, their peers or colleagues in other departments and organisations."

Vanessa recognises that things are changing but that agents of change are not always in the right place. People at the top of an organisation might recognise the need for culture change and more junior staff may push for it, but a key band of managers in the middle are not yet going along.

"I think there is still what they call the 'marzipan layer' in organisations that nod at new suggestions but do nothing and almost sabotage some of this stuff. If you are in a lower part of the organisation, you might be hearing the right noises but nothing is getting done.

"That centre band is where the focus needs to be because they are the ones that can make stuff happen. They have got money, they have got influence, they are feeding the upper layers and they are nurturing the lower layers. I think middle management has a hell of a lot to answer for and they are the change makers for me."

Are Women More Comfortable Sharing With Other Women?

When looking at the question of gender differences in asking for help, I was struck by a comment made by Hillary Clinton in her 2017 book *What Happened*[23]. Clinton talked about to whom she turns for help and support, who challenges and encourages her. While she has men in her circle who play a key role, she was at pains to point out 'My girlfriends are something else entirely. In my experience, there's a special strength at the heart of friendships between women. We get real with each other. We talk about raw and painful things. We admit to each other insecurities and fears that we sometimes don't admit even to ourselves.'

I wanted to explore whether women are more comfortable opening up to other women or would they be just as comfortable in the company of men. And what about men?

Inspired by a book by Zella King and Amanda Scott[24], Vanessa has her own mastermind group, a 'Personal Boardroom' with a small group of women who provide her with support and a sounding board for new ideas.

"They are at my level, it's OK to fail having them around me. I have always worked with men and I have always run male teams, so it has been a complete change for me running female teams and calling on those advocates to be women.

"My supporters were men in the past and they gave me the grounding to do what I do today. But I think having that sounding board is so important. Women who have got my back, women who will open up doors of opportunity in an instant. They also provide me with a safe space to download my fears."

Luke told me that gender does play a role in whom men like to share with as well but there is more at play. "I find that blokes do prefer to speak to other men but I think it's got to be the right man for them. Men or women, people relate back to people who have been through what they have been through.

Men or women, people relate back to people who have been through what they have been through.

"If you are someone who can sit and explain to someone what you have gone through and they have gone through it, male or female, that other person sitting across from you will get more out of it."

21.

Is It Harder for Introverts to Ask for Help?

M any of the stories in this book centre on people sharing their challenges and allowing other people to help them. It's inevitable that personality type plays an important role in whether people are comfortable doing this. If someone is more introverted, does it follow that it is harder for them to open up?

I spoke with Jennifer B Kahnweiler, an expert on helping organisations harness the power of introverts and the author of several books including *Quiet Influence*, *The Introverted Leader* and *The Genius of Opposites*.

"Extroverts tend to talk out their thoughts," Jennifer told me. "They don't self-censure, whereas introverts think more before they speak and tend not to speak up because of this internal self-talk.

Introverts think more before they speak and tend not to speak up because of this internal self-talk.

"While this reflection is a strength, when you overuse a strength it can become a weakness. Thinking too much and overanalysing can prevent introverts from engaging in the natural ebb and flow of conversations.

"Introverts don't necessarily ease into talking about their needs, desires and what they're looking for. Introverts tell me that natural repartee is not as easy for them as it is for extroverts, who can often get anyone to talk. For introverts, even small talk has to be planned.

"I believe that introverts possess one of the greatest skills required to network effectively: being great at engaged listening. When they listen, they learn about people and find themselves in a position to offer support and help based on what they are hearing. When they take the time to delve deeper with people in one-on-one conversation, they build trust. It is then that they are more comfortable asking for what they themselves need."

Persistent and Intentional

If it sounds as though the advantage in personality type is all one way, Jennifer was adamant that extroverts aren't great at asking for help and support either. "Extroverts talk a lot but it doesn't necessarily correlate that they ask for more support, certainly not directly.

"Whether you are an introvert or extrovert, being assertive is about knowing what you need and asking for it while respecting the other person's needs. It is also about being persistent and intentional.

"Introverts naturally plan and prepare and they can be incredibly effective in asking for what they need and want. Networking is a process of mutual exchange, so introverts can think about what they want, ask for it and also offer to help others. Asking for what you need is a skill and any skill takes practise to perfect. If you are not asking for help, it becomes overwhelming when you have to and it erodes your confidence."

Of course, a lack of confidence is not necessarily a quality unique to introverts. In fact, many introverts feel confident in many areas of their life but just don't enjoy being in the spotlight, while for many extroverts the spotlight helps them to hide their true vulnerabilities in plain sight.

For many extroverts the spotlight helps them to hide their true vulnerabilities in plain sight.

In fact, are there ways in which introverts can benefit from a more considered approach to asking for the support of their network than extroverts?

Futurist and strategy consultant Graeme Codrington, an introvert himself, told me that he believes that to be the case. "For me, the big difference between an introvert and an extrovert is that the extrovert has lots of surface level connections, whereas the introvert has fewer but much deeper relationships. I can see the value of both, so I wouldn't want to say that an introvert is better, because when I need help or want to open up to people, I've got a much smaller group I can go to but I think I can get more from those people than an extrovert might.

"When I open up to somebody, they probably are so surprised that they take me a lot more seriously than they might take my brother, for example, who is the complete opposite. My brother could probably access more people but I think he would get a lower level of engagement than I would."

My brother could probably access more people but I think he would get a lower level of engagement than I would.

My business strapline is 'Connecting is not Enough' and my driver for over 20 years speaking and writing about professional relationships has been to get across the message that it's not a numbers game. Quality of conversation and depth of relationship count for much more than breadth of network.

Just because you don't have a vast network doesn't mean that the support you need is not still readily available to you. In fact, the support you receive from a small but deep network may well be richer and more impactful.

Leadership Qualities

Jennifer believes that a good manager can help introverts to find the help they need.

"I recently talked with scientists at a multinational pharmaceutical company about how they can start to get their ideas out there.

They said they have a lot of issues with people being introverted and not sharing their thoughts in meetings. The researchers believe that it's affecting the kinds of drugs they are bringing to market. They need *everybody's* input.

"Strong leadership is critically important in situations like these. Leaders can play the role of finding out from people what they need by asking 'How can I support you?'

"The best leaders build trust individually, they get off the email chains, they meet one to one and get to know people and encourage them and help grow their careers.

"It's nothing that we don't know but I keep hearing it from both sides − introverts just want people to take the time to recognise them. Don't expect introverts to change to suit you; a good leader needs to make it comfortable for people to want to come to them."

22.

Is Modern Life Changing the Way Younger Generations Share?

Many of my conversations about vulnerability in our professional lives have led back to how younger generations coming into work now and over the next few years will have a different mindset and expectations, causing the culture in the workplace to shift.

The Millennial generation are now part of the workforce and older Generation Z are not far behind. Facebook was founded in 2004, launching globally in 2006, which means that many people born after 2000 will have experienced social media as a core part of their identity and communication for much of their teens.

That will almost certainly lead to a different approach to communication compared to Baby Boomers and Generation X, who grew up with a rotary phone on the hall table and writing letters to each other. I wanted to find out more about how all of these changes impact on the way younger generations open up to each other, so I spoke with my 21-year-old niece, Samantha.

Sam is an undergraduate at the University of Birmingham, studying Liberal Arts and Sciences. When I spoke with her, Sam and her fellow students had just completed a study on loneliness among youth[25], exploring whether today's young people are the loneliest generation ever.

Sam told me, "We found that more young people are lonely than any other generation, partly because we do not really talk to each other anymore. A lot of the emphasis on loneliness has been around elderly people because they often end up living by themselves. Actually, young people are still lonelier because it is far too easy nowadays to not speak to people in person. We hide behind a phone and we live our lives through that rather than enjoying actual human contact."

We hide behind a phone and we live our lives through that rather than enjoying actual human contact.

I challenged Sam, asking whether social media can allow us to communicate more widely and consistently than before. While there are clear issues with spending too much time engaged on phones when in company, can't social media encourage more sharing and communication at other times?

"Social media is great in some ways. When I was travelling and meeting a lot of people around the world, I managed to stay in touch with them, which you could not do so easily 30 years ago. But when you speak to people online it is a different type of conversation. When you speak to people in person you cannot undo or delete stuff that you do not mean to say or take time to plan the best response; it is just what comes out of your mouth in the moment.

When you speak to people in person you cannot undo or delete stuff that you do not mean to say or take time to plan the best response.

"It is different to having a real-life conversation with someone. The research that we did showed that people aged 18 to 24 are twenty times more likely to never speak to their neighbours than those aged 55 because we are losing the skill of human interaction.

"Our face-to-face communication skills are disappearing. When you speak to someone online you are missing 90% of the conversation and a lot of the time body language and tone convey how you are feeling. It is very easy to message someone and say 'Having a great time!' They cannot see you or hear you and so they take that comment at surface value.

"If you said that in person, they might be able to tell by how you are talking and what you are doing that it is not true. Then they can get you to open up. People are not talking about struggles with mental health issues or lack of self-esteem because other people do not know that they are struggling. We are not seeing each other in the same way."

Social Perfectionism

The perfect image being shared through our online communication documented elsewhere in this book is also impacting the ability of younger generations to share. In terms of self-image, social media is one of the worst things, particularly for a teenage girl.

For Sam, the growth of social media has left her and her friends with greater challenges than her parents' or grandparents' generations. The impact on the way we communicate and engage with each other has been huge.

"Growing up is always hard; I am not saying that people who grew up 60 years ago did not have a tough time with puberty and adolescence and everything that goes with that. But social media is one of the biggest changes that we have experienced as a society and it has a massive impact on your life from the moment you are exposed to it. I think my age group was quite lucky in that when I was very young it was not around.

"When I got to 12 or 13, Facebook happened, then Instagram, Snapchat. I remember Snapchat starting, I was maybe 13 or 14. My cousin is 12; she had an iPhone when she was five and was looking up Facebook and Instagram. She was exposed at a very young age to that kind of perfectionism and heavy influence.

"Everything you do now is photographed and undoubtedly you will post one of those pictures on social media and you will get whatever number of likes, then someone that you know will get more likes than you. That is what we are growing up with now. That is what we are used to. I try very hard to ignore it. It is a sad truth now that we are completely obsessed; we are more obsessed with what people online will think than whether we feel good about ourselves.

"There was a study in the States and the UK[26] that analysed university-aged students over the course of 25 years and measured how they rated themselves on a perfectionism scale. The findings said that younger generations were the ones who were struggling more and more with this social perfectionism, where we feel we have to be perfect in every aspect of our life.

"It is that need to reach standards that are unreasonably high and unrealistic and to measure up to other people which social media has made practically impossible."

Talking About Mental Health

When I told people I was planning to write this book, the increase in depression and other mental health issues among young people was frequently mentioned. Sam's perspective on the challenges of social perfectionism and of constantly living up to idealised lifestyles seem to point to a possible reason for this surge.

Sam thinks that the increased focus on mental health is a double-edged sword. "In a way we are getting better and getting worse at the same time because the dialogue around mental health has massively expanded recently. At the same time there are a lot of people who will say that a person does not actually have depression, they are just saying it because it is the 'in' thing.

"My issue with that is you do not know that person so you cannot judge. The thing now is that everyone is struggling with their mental health, which is true. Mental health is like physical health, you are hardly going to be perfect your whole life, that is impossible.

"There are some brilliant role models posting lots of stuff about how it is OK to have a bad day or sharing their struggle with depression, anxiety or an eating disorder. But there are many who feel like they cannot talk about it until they are out of it. A lot of people will look at role models sharing the depression they have overcome and think 'but you are out of it now, it is easy for you to say this was easy or this was hard'. Then there are also people who will post and say 'I struggle with depression and it is really difficult'. Someone who struggles with depression might realise that they are not alone.

"Feeling alone is what causes so many problems."

Feeling alone is what causes so many problems.

23.

ARE THERE CULTURAL DIFFERENCES IN OUR WILLINGNESS TO OPEN UP AND ASK FOR HELP?

Throughout this book I have tried to illustrate the concept of opening up and asking for help through the experiences of a range of people from around the world. One question is left for us to look at though. How strongly do the cultures we grow up with influence our willingness to be honest about our shortcomings?

I am often asked for my thoughts on cultural differences when it comes to networking. There are certainly differences in approach but, in my experience, many of these come down to accepted etiquette rather than something deeper. Perhaps people are more trusting in Western than Eastern Europe and more conscious of seniority in South East Asia, but I have found that when you speak to people individually we have more in common than you might expect.

When you speak to people individually, we have more in common than you might expect.

I wanted to explore whether it is the same when it comes to vulnerability. How much do cultures differ in regards to sharing? And to what extent are those differences purely at a surface level? It is important to bear in mind that cultural differences are far more widespread and nuanced than the brief regional overview presented here.

Is Vulnerability Seen as a Weakness?

I began by seeking to understand the impact of patriarchal cultures on sharing. My assumption going into these conversations was that cultures with a more male-oriented tradition, with a strong expectation of the male leader and hunter-gatherer, would create an environment that frowned upon vulnerability.

Gil Petersil is a successful Israeli entrepreneur who has operated businesses all over the world, most recently in Russia and Singapore. Gil was clear that he saw a difference in the attitude towards such transparency in different countries, particularly in the entrepreneur community.

Gil told me, "In some cultures, in the United States and Israel especially, people in the startup industry know that vulnerability equals power. They know that vulnerability shows that you are open to mentorship; you are open to advice, open to receive help.

Vulnerability equals power. Vulnerability shows that you are open to mentorship; you are open to advice, open to receive help.

"In places like Russia, the Middle East and some places in Asia it is a sign of weakness. Being vulnerable and telling people you failed at something or you are not strong enough tends to be seen in a negative way. In Russia for example, most entrepreneurs would never show signs of weakness because they think someone else will step all over them.

"This is very much connected to historic Russian pride; being strong men you cannot show weakness. This is why a lot of businesses in Russia have so many simple problems that could be easily resolved but they do not ask for help."

Oscar Onyema, the CEO of the Nigerian Stock Exchange, sees different national characteristics across Africa but certainly recognises the importance of masculine strength in determining people's willingness to share in his home country. "If you looked at Nigerians generally," he told me, "the stereotype is that they are 'out there' as opposed to people from some other African countries who are perceived as more reserved.

"Because we have this macho 'can do' attitude, it is harder for people to put out their vulnerabilities and ask for help. That would be a general statement from a Nigerian perspective. Whereas from a country like Kenya or Zimbabwe you are more likely to get people asking for help."

Oscar sees the Nigerian failure to ask for help as a major issue, potentially leading to a poorer standard of workmanship and an inability to progress. "I don't see a lot of change, what I do see are people becoming very passive," he said.

"Even workmen in Nigeria think they know when they don't really know and they are not using tools that they have been trained on. They would rather try to do it by hand. Even when they have learned new techniques, they do not apply what they have learned."

Media entrepreneur Apurva Purohit also sees traditional cultural norms in India acting as a barrier to genuine transparency and openness. "I think men find it extremely difficult," she told me. "It is not expected of them. They are supposed to be the breadwinner, the mountain of strength. We look for the guy who does not show emotion, who is good in a crisis and unflappable. That is a stereotype that has been thrust upon them. It is very clear that asking for help will be seen as a weakness."

Saving Face

Another cultural expectation that strongly impacts on people's willingness to share is the Asian culture of 'Face'. My experience of working with both Western and Chinese businesses in Asia has taught me the difference between the two cultures the hard way and one thing that I had to learn quickly was the importance of maintaining Face.

I asked Ruth Lau, a Chinese banker and Harvard alumnus, to help me better understand Face.

Ruth told me, "Face is something so important to many Chinese people that it can be more important than their lives. They would rather die than lose Face. It is more than just dignity; I think it's too simple to translate it as dignity. It's almost the honour of the whole family.

"I know lots of very poor families who don't have money to buy food for their children but they have to send packets with money to people they don't know because they are getting married. This is all to do with very old traditions."

The concept of Face clearly makes sharing a weakness or concern very difficult. Ruth told me, "It becomes really tough to be honest and authentic. People will want to cover up; they will never want other people to know that they are not doing well."

Ruth experienced the difficulties posed by the fear of losing Face when her first marriage was going badly. She told me, "I can share failures when I'm with Western people, I feel comfortable because I know people won't judge me. But with Chinese people I wouldn't. I can't just tell my mum or tell other people 'I've failed', this is something they can't accept.

I can share failures when I'm with Western people, I feel comfortable because I know people won't judge me. But with Chinese people I wouldn't.

"In a way I really feel the power of being authentic when I share with Western friends. If you're authentic in the short term you might lose but in the long term you always gain."

Knowing Your Place

Singaporean author Wendy Tan Siew Inn believes that there is a cultural conflict that makes it hard for business leaders and influencers to seek support. She told me, "I think there are two dimensions here.

"In the Asian culture we see ourselves as humble, needing to learn from others. So, this sense of humility makes it normal to ask for help. At the same time, if this person sees himself as the expert, or is perceived as the leader in the organisation, then it is harder to ask for help because of the need to maintain Face. The expectation is probably still for the leader to know what to do, to have thought it out."

"I would advise leaders to seek counsel from people they trust and, after drawing from different perspectives, formulate their own strategy and then share it with the people they are leading."

This sense of people knowing their place and seeking advice from people who are older, more experienced or who are perceived as wiser is not prevalent just in Chinese culture. Oscar mentioned the importance of hierarchies when asking for help in African cultures too.

He told me, "If you are a giver in Nigeria, you're perceived to be superior to the person who is receiving. People would typically ask for help from people they perceive as stronger or richer."

This challenges some of the findings from John Jameson's pilot study discussed in chapter 6, where senior executives were found to show more self-compassion which, in turn, led to greater vulnerability.

If you look more closely, perhaps there is not a direct contradiction and this may be a cultural indicator. In Jameson's study, more senior people were seen to be more confident in their own decisions.

Perhaps that shows up in some cultures as more willingness to discuss the way forward with others, while in others it leads to a more closed approach.

Opening Up

Germans are often thought of as very direct and Sustainable Leadership expert Niels Brabandt is the most direct German I know. Niels is a man of few words and the ones he uses are rarely sugar coated. I wanted to find out if he felt that his approach was typically Germanic and understand his willingness to support people who asked for help.

Niels told me that while he could see a generational shift and an increase in the number of people asking for help publicly, it is generally more expected that people will open up to their family and close friends but not to a wider circle. Niels said, "Nine out of ten Germans will see it as a weakness when you publicly ask for help.

"I would never go to even a good client of mine and say, 'I'm struggling businesswise and I need help'. That would make me lose the mandate. Family, friends, yes, but you'd turn to a small circle of close people rather than a large circle of people who you barely know."

Niels does a lot of work in the UK and he sees a big difference between the way British people and Germans ask for help. "British people are, in my opinion, a lot more open. In Germany we are very cautious, especially where I am from in northern Germany. We are not known to be particularly talkative. We are quite selective about who we talk to and what we talk about, so we are a lot more closed in the way we handle our issues. The better people know me and the better I know them, the more direct I am. That is a very northern German approach."

In return, Niels expects people to be very direct with him on the occasions when he does ask for help. Not for him the 'praise sandwich' of compliment-critique-compliment favoured by many in US and UK self-development circles. He just wants the basic facts that he can work with.

"I want people to challenge my ideas. I don't put an idea in front of them to hear how great it is. When I put the idea out there, I obviously think it's pretty good. When I ask for feedback on a piece of work, I tell people, 'Don't tell me what you liked, everything you do not mention was obviously OK. Only tell me what I need to improve'."

Wendy believes that in Asia, too, the relationship between people is central to how appropriate it is to ask for or offer help. The deeper the relationship, the easier it is, particularly if support is unsolicited. I think that this is the case in other parts of the world too but easily overlooked as some people focus on getting what they can or impressing others rather than investing in strong, mutually supportive relationships.

"I would say that in the Chinese Asian context, a lot of it has to do with the level of trust in a relationship. Have I built a relationship to the extent where I have implicit permission to give advice, feedback, or suggest something that wasn't solicited?

"There is a Chinese saying 'Bao-Rong' which means you embrace each other's flaws. If you look at divorce rates, in the West they are higher because people are more assertive about what they want whereas in Asia we are more willing to put up with our differences.

There is a Chinese saying 'Bao-Rong' which means you embrace each other's flaws.

"Sometimes the relationship and sense of responsibility to others is more important than asserting our rights or pursuing our freedom. We accept the other party for who he is or we tolerate and accept differences."

Sepehr Tarverdian is an experienced Iranian events industry executive with business interests across the Middle East. Sepehr told me that in Iran people are very careful about who they help, particularly in business. "People are not willing to ask for support; they want to do things for themselves. I rarely find people asking for help from others because most Iranians will not help you anyway. When I have problems myself, I don't call others either."

We are Family

One common thread I found in all of the conversations I had was the importance of family. The word 'family' is taken more literally in some cultures than others and can extend from immediate relations to people who you spend most of your time with irrespective of blood ties. Whatever your definition, it is most people's primary source of advice and support.

For Siberian Natalya Khornauhova, family definitely comes first. "Russian traditions are very family oriented," Natalya told me. "The big difference from Western people is that Russian people do not go to experts. If you go to seek help from experts, such as therapists, that would be perceived as something being seriously wrong.

"It seems abnormal not to talk to your parents. We tend to stay closer to people; my sister, for example, lives next door. This is the way that seems comfortable in Russia. Even when we move far away, we often try to bring our parents with us."

Families may be close in Russia but Natalya perceives that trust outside that close circle has diminished since the fall of the Soviet Union. She believes that capitalism has brought with it a change in behaviour that has adversely affected relationships outside family circles. It is something that I have heard in other former Soviet countries as well.

"People were much more open, everyone knew what was happening with their neighbour, you knew all your neighbours and your door was never locked. Never. Capitalism has come, people think differently and they behave in a different way. They are locking themselves to a very small circle of people that they can actually trust."

Gil believes that Russian culture needs to shift and wants to see much more sharing between people outside the family. He told me, "If you look at the average person in Russia, they are extremely open with their families. Open to a degree that their mother tends to be the mentor, their sister tends to be their best friend.

If you look at the average person in Russia, they are extremely open with their families. Open to a degree that their mother tends to be the mentor, their sister tends to be their best friend.

"The Russian culture of always being open to family is nice but it is not necessarily what is needed when you have to make difficult decisions in life. Especially the parents of today's younger generation in Russia. They lived during the Soviet era, in a world where their minds were completely set on not planning into the future and doing things for yourself. It is a completely different mindset from what the younger generation is focused on these days."

Gil sees the shift from communism to capitalism in a different way from Natalya and, in particular, sees the influence of Russia opening up to the rest of the world having a key influence in big cities. "Under communism you did not have a reason to not trust, things were so closed that you did not need to network and make new connections.

"Big cities like Moscow and St Petersburg are both populated and visited by many foreigners. They are affected by collaboration, joint ventures and partnerships. The rest of the world is rubbing off on them."

While there may be less that separates us than some people might contend, there are still clear differences, even on a fairly local basis. As people like Oscar, Sepehr and Ruth were all at pains to point out, there are huge differences in cultures within regions and within countries. For example, Natalya and Gil's perspectives on Russian culture may be strongly influenced by where they spend their time – Natalya in Siberia and Gil in Moscow and St Petersburg.

From my own experience I would venture that there are cultural differences even within a country as small as the UK. When I interviewed Phil Gardner, he talked about the difference in approach between northerners and southerners in England and I would also argue that family and educational background and life experience are just as likely to influence your approach to sharing as where you were born and raised. It is important, therefore, to be aware of these differences and sensitive to others' personal comfort and style when seeking to engage with them or encourage them to share.

If you want to either ask for help or offer support to someone in your network, the key is to be aware of their willingness to engage. Culture may be one factor in their approach but it won't be the only one. Other influences, such as their level of introversion, past experiences (most of which it's unlikely you'll be aware of), education and upbringing will all play a role in how people respond.

Yes, there are certain cultural styles we need to be respectful of, but treat everyone individually in a way that you feel they will be comfortable with and you should be on firm ground.

Section Six

The Way Forward

24.

What Stops Us From Sharing and What Can We Do About It?

You might assume that it would be the most natural thing in the world to ask for help and turn to others for support. We are not, after all, a solitary species by nature. Community and tribe lie at the core of human behaviour and overwhelmingly we seek the comfort of a mate. So why do some people go to extremes to take their biggest challenges and heaviest burdens on themselves?

I spoke with Johanna Jameson, a licensed clinical professional counsellor in Chicago and Dr Lynda Shaw, a neuroscientist and business psychologist in the UK, to try to understand just why we respond in the way we do.

Johanna agreed with my premise that we are driven by connection. She told me, "It is a very human need to want to connect to others, feel loved, have someone to share our life experiences with. But it is also survival. We all want to feel we belong. We want to feel we belong in society, we belong with our family, we belong in a job. It is a basic principle."

We all want to feel we belong. We want to feel we belong in society, we belong with our family, we belong in a job.

Lynda also recognised community as a fundamental human need but is concerned that we are letting our natural tendency to congregate slip away. Many communities have fragmented due to the nature of modern life and Lynda pointed to some of the dwindling traditional communities still in existence as an illustration of what we are missing. Natalya's observations in the last chapter on life in Siberia illustrate the gaps Lynda sees elsewhere.

"In the modern day we are more isolated because you do not get families living together like we used to. You do not get grandparents looking after grandchildren while parents go to work with everyone living under the same roof. In Germany they used to extend their houses all the time for the next generation coming in. It does not happen anymore.

"Even in Indian and Pakistani communities in the UK, families are starting to spread out. Where they have always been very strong, close-knit family units, the kids are moving away to work and communities are breaking up.

"There are five very different places in the world known as Blue Zones[27]. They are Okinawa in Japan, Sardinia in Italy, Nicoya in Costa Rica, Ikaria in Greece and the Seven Day Adventist community in Loma Linda, California. They have five generations of people in a family living healthily; no heart disease, no dementia, no high blood pressure. Scientists continue to visit these communities to understand what they are doing right.

"One of the key findings was that they eat around the table together as a family every day. They have a very strong social connection. We are not meant to be isolated. We are meant to embrace one another."

Modern Life

So, what has changed? Are we turning away from communities and the support they provide because of the pressures of modern life or is it something else?

It's not a simple answer – there are a number of factors – but the 21st-century lifestyle certainly doesn't seem to be encouraging us to hold on to our traditional support structures.

Johanna sees a stark contrast between life in the Blue Zones and modern-day life in her hometown of Chicago. "Icaria is known as The Island of No Time. They do not have any clocks and they just get on with their day.

The 21st-century lifestyle certainly doesn't seem to be encouraging us to hold on to our traditional support structures.

"Compare that to living in Chicago where it is hustle and bustle. You're always focused on your next meeting; you do not really sit down to enjoy the person in front of you. We are on our phones all the time. In a place like Icaria they do not have that worry. They are all about connecting, sitting down and having tea with their neighbours. Our daily society really doesn't allow us the time to connect on that level."

Lynda told me that as we move away from communities, people are spending more time in their own company and that is a key factor in our drive to solve problems for ourselves. Something that she admits to falling prey to herself.

"There is natural erosion going on. When things go wrong some people have a mentality of locking themselves away to sort it out. I am one of those. If I have got a big problem, I do not want to talk about it. I want to fix it – then I will talk about it."

Too Guilty to Share

Lynda mentioned two key factors that prevent people from sharing that I hadn't considered before our conversation but which made perfect sense to me.

Lynda told me, "There is an element of shame and also an element of guilt. Freud said that one of the underpinnings of depression is guilt. We are now talking about it because in neuroscience we are seeing that the emotion of guilt is apparent with people with depression.

"Often people with clinical depression think that they haven't got a reason to be depressed so they feel guilty about it, especially if they consider themselves to have a privileged upbringing or environment. They see people who have had a really tough time who are not clinically depressed and they struggle with that."

Johanna recognises the same issues and sees them every day in her therapy sessions. "There are some people who cannot control their depression, it is chemical. As Lynda said, they see other people going through something way worse and who don't suffer in the same way.

"Most of my clients just come to me and say 'I am so sorry I am bothering you with this. I am wasting your time; this is not a big deal. I know there are other people suffering far more than me'. I think that is an idea that gets put out there; you have to tough it out, there are a lot of other people suffering in the world.

I think that is an idea that gets put out there; you have to tough it out, there are a lot of other people suffering in the world.

"That might be another way in which being so connected affects our willingness to share. People see all these horrible things happening and say 'Why am I asking for help? I should be able to deal with this on my own, it is not that bad when you look at the world around us'."

Deliciously Imperfect

As we have seen in many of the stories in this book, particularly those of Dawnna and Pegine, any of the decisions we take in life are the result of learned behaviour. We take on board past experiences and the lessons we have drawn from them and they influence actions we take in the future. For both Johanna and Lynda, these past experiences account for many of the reasons why we don't ask for help.

Johanna shared an extreme (if sadly not uncommon) example to make the point. "It is something we often see in children that come from abusive families. Their experience in love and affection is damaged, so they are taught that being vulnerable and reaching out for connection is a bad thing. As a result, as they go through their adult life they avoid that.

"From a counselling standpoint you see that all the time; those fears that people have could stem from something that happened in early childhood or it could be something later in life, like getting your dream job and then losing it."

To tackle this learned behaviour, professionals like Johanna and Lynda work with clients on increasing their self-worth and resilience, subtly reprogramming their memories and thought processes to turn those negative memories into something positive.

"When I am in therapy with someone," says Johanna, "the first thing I start with is trying to find a strength. It could be something so small: you think you are going through a struggle but you got out of bed this morning? You just have to look for it, it is there."

In the pilot research that we undertook for this book (chapter 6) we saw how self-compassion increased participants' willingness to ask for help. The work on resilience that Johanna and Lynda shared with me is all focused on increasing that self-compassion.

Lynda explained, "If you are feeling compassion for yourself, if you like yourself as a human being, I think you create empathy for others. When you have empathy for others many things fall into place. In actual fact we are deliciously imperfect. And once we are aware of these things and like ourselves regardless, we become better human beings and we start embracing others more and communicate better. We will ask for help more because we will not feel so bad about it."

*We are deliciously imperfect. And once we are aware of these
things and like ourselves regardless, we become better human
beings and we start embracing others more.*

Who Should We Share With?

I started this chapter by looking at our natural inclination to share
within our communities and how that has possibly fallen away.
Despite this, there is still a stronger drive to share with family than
anyone else, as I found out in my exploration of different cultural
approaches to sharing (chapter 23). But is there a role for sharing
with strangers?

Lynda and Johanna both agreed that they would not personally
choose to share their deepest vulnerabilities with complete strangers
and they both have a range of people in their close networks in
whom they will confide. But, unsurprisingly perhaps, they both felt
that therapists play an important role too, irrespective of whether
or not anything is clinically wrong.

Johanna told me, "Therapy is not just there if you have a diagnosis
of clinical depression or if you're bipolar. Life is hard, we all
struggle. There is a point in everyone's life where you need to talk
to someone who is not a friend, not family, to just get that unbiased
opinion and support. You might not be able to turn that corner
without looking for the help that you need.

"But everyone's journey is so different. There are some people who
say you can get over it on your own, it really just depends on the
level of complexity of the issue."

The culture people come from will influence people's willingness to talk to a therapist. It often seems, looking from the outside, that therapy is seen as far more of an everyday service in the United States than in many other cultures. Compare that to the comments of Natalya Khornauhova in chapter 23 who said that in Russia people think that there is something seriously wrong with you if you talk to a therapist.

Johanna recognises these differences. "I think it really depends on the person. I get some people who always surprise me with what they share and they will say things like 'You are the first person I have told this to'."

Lynda argues that there are times when opening up to a stranger who is a professional helps to preserve the equilibrium elsewhere in your life.

"In a family you have got dynamics you do not want to change. That stands with mental health issues. Some people feel comfortable about sharing these things with their family, other people prefer a stranger. They prefer to share with someone for whom it is their job, there is no emotional attachment and they are not going to be rocking the boat in terms of the dynamics with those at home."

25.

How Will Technology Impact Our Tendency or Need to Share and be Open?

From the bare-all perfect world of social media platforms to rapidly changing business models, technology is a key tool in encouraging us to share more widely. Rapid technological changes are affecting all of us, individually, organisationally and in our communities.

I asked three experts on predicting future economic and demographic trends for their perspective on how recent advances have impacted us and whether they are likely to do so in the future.

South African Graeme Codrington believes that social media has played a tremendous role in changing our social landscape. One of the biggest shifts he has seen is one towards openness. He told me, "One of the reasons is the general transparency that the internet and social media bring. I mean that in a good way, the transparency of knowing a little more about each other, our colleagues' personal lives for example, because you can follow them on Facebook.

"Increased transparency has enabled people to recognise that they are not the only person going through a particular issue. It's meant that people have felt more comfortable openly talking about their personal challenges with colleagues.

Increased transparency has enabled people to recognise that they are not the only person going through a particular issue.

"They might not throw it out on social media but people generally feel safer now talking about struggling with depression or other issues than they may have done 20 years ago. At the other end of the scale, it also has magnified online bullying. Some people have taken the chance to be vulnerable and then been shot down in that vulnerability. Rather than being either good or bad, it's been very good and very bad simultaneously."

Adapting to the Changing World of Work

Global futurist Rohit Talwar believes that technology is leading change in the world of work and we need leaders in government and business to change their mindset. A lack of vulnerability is not just an individual issue, it can affect an organisation as well.

"All of the changes that are disrupting various global governance systems and markets are coming as a shock to leaders," Rohit explained. "We are seeing lots of governments struggle with change and businesses fail.

"Leaders need to accept that they do not understand the different mindsets, business models and technology that have changed their landscape and seen their customers go elsewhere. There is a lack of willingness to admit that we do not understand.

Leaders need to accept that they do not understand the different mindsets, business models and technology that have changed their landscape.

"Changes like Artificial Intelligence (AI) are going to challenge our world. AI is moving so fast and the potential is becoming clearer. Any organisation that does not have an active process of investigating it is really putting its future on the line. Like many other exponentially advancing technologies, AI is going to penetrate every aspect of our world and we need to understand it and take steps to experiment with it, embrace it, and try stuff that might fail.

"That is a very vulnerable approach – to be going to our employees, our partners, our shareholders and explaining that we have to experiment and that we need to invest more in our learning, starting from the top. It is not a sign of weakness, it is actually a massive sign of strength that we acknowledge what we do not know and that we are going out to learn."

Former IBM Global Managing Partner Andrew Grill also sees major changes in the workspace but believes technology can play a key role in identifying issues with employees where previously they may have bottled things up.

"I'm wearing a Fitbit and you're probably wearing an Apple Watch," Andrew observed. "We are already instrumenting ourselves in such a way that maybe AI is going to tell us 'We don't think you're OK today'. You may outwardly say 'I'm feeling fine' but the tech is going to send a message to a manager saying that you are at 50% today.

"At the moment I use a couple of apps; I use Fitbit and I use an app called Gyroscope that pulls everything together including how much time I spend on my computer, where I go, it even asks me about my mood once a day.

"As human beings I don't think we will change, it will continue to be seen as a negative to say to someone that you are having a bad day, that you are depressed or unhappy. Perhaps we can use technology to sensitively tell someone else that we need assistance or that our performance is compromised."

Perhaps we can use technology to sensitively tell someone else that we need assistance or that our performance is compromised.

Many people will be uncomfortable with such a scenario and there are a lot of concerns about how much information we already share through technology and how that data is used. Governments and large organisations now have access to more personal information than ever before and Rohit believes that this could have tremendous repercussions in the future.

"China is doing a lot of good stuff with tech but it is also doing things that should concern us. Social scoring is a good example, where they have started to rank individuals based on whether they are doing the 'right things'.

"That is where you start to worry about how technology-enabled 24/7 surveillance could erode personal freedom in the future. It might actually mitigate against people being vulnerable or being curious. You may see a massive increase in governments and businesses starting to force everyone to conform to a very narrow set of norms. Then I think society will become less creative and less imaginative, less open and less capable of responding to future shocks."

26.

THE RULES OF ASKING

The journey we have taken has crisscrossed the globe and seen us share a range of experiences from professional to the deeply personal. But there are common threads running through all those experiences.

We have seen how the support of networks has helped people through tough times, how easy it is to develop a veneer of invulnerability and the importance of accepting that we're not perfect. We are better off if we allow other people to support us and we need to work together to encourage others to open up so that we can support them.

It's not easy to ask though. As I draw this book to a close, here are ten Rules of Asking that I hope will help you on your own journey and allow you to both ask for and receive support in times of need.

Rule 1 – Understand What is Stopping You

We Don't Want to be a Burden to Others – Probably the primary blocker to asking for help is that we don't want to be a nuisance. Well, let me ask you something. When was the last time you helped someone you care about? If it worked out, how did it make you feel?

When I ask those questions in talks and seminars, most people respond positively to the second question. They felt 'great', 'happy', 'delighted', 'awesome'.

So, we feel great when we help others but we don't ask for help for ourselves because we don't want to be a burden. Can you see the disconnect here? By not asking people who trust and love us, we are denying them the pleasure of seeing us succeed.

By not asking people who trust and love us, we are denying them the pleasure of seeing us succeed.

We don't want to appear vulnerable – If you're worried about looking weak when you ask, reframe the question. Instead of telling people that you don't know what to do, tell them that you have ideas but would appreciate their input. Instead of telling people that you are struggling, tell them that you think you could do more and ask for their feedback.

And remember, being courageous enough to ask for help is a strength, not a weakness.

We assume that they can't or won't want to help – Understand that a refusal to help will often not be about you, there may be a number of reasons why people can't help you. They may be too busy, they may be supporting others, they may not feel that they are qualified to help. In fact, if you're asking people who know, like and trust you, it's very unlikely that any refusal will be a reflection on you.

Rule 2 – Stop Worrying About Looking Good

We need to park our ego to one side and let others help us if we are to achieve our highest potential. Accept that you can make mistakes and that everyone else can as well.

I was particularly struck by the report by the team at Harvard Business School outlined in chapter 15 exploring how we respond better to people who share their failures than those who only talk about their successes. They told me that when leaders don't share, their staff remain unaware of their struggles on their journey to success.

Rule 3 – Make it Easy for People to Help You

Be willing to hear 'no' without taking it negatively or personally and be open to brutal feedback and to hearing things you're not comfortable with.

Be willing to hear 'no' without taking it negatively or personally.

Be very clear about the help that you're looking for and don't be afraid to bring people back on track if you feel that they have missed the point. As long as you respect yourself and respect the people supporting you, you should be able to have open and honest conversations.

As well as helping people to support us individually, we can all play our part in making it easier for us to help each other collectively. Among our friends, our community and in our workplaces, let's make it acceptable to ask for help and ensure that everybody feels confident that they won't be judged adversely for doing so.

Finally, make it not just easy but a pleasure for people to help you.

Rule 4 – Be Authentic

Rather than dismissing 'authenticity' as a buzzword, I think it is important to understand why this term keeps coming up.

Let others know if you are finding things tough and be honest about what you are going through. The trouble with wearing a mask is that it can become heavy and uncomfortable after a while. Once you have tackled the uncomfortable issues you can start to focus on solutions. In a world where social media seems to encourage us to present the best side of ourselves and compete for the perfect life, an authentic voice will stand out even more above the noise.

Rule 5 – Be Timely

The longer you leave things before you ask for help, the deeper the hole you'll dig for yourself. Don't prevaricate; if you need answers, ideas or support, reach out and ask.

One simple thing you can do to make sure that you are focused on asking for help is to diarise one time each month to do so. Identify your biggest challenge at that moment and consider who you know who might provide valuable insight. Who has the expertise, experience, contacts or different perspective that could be relevant to that problem? It might be one person, it might be three or four. Tell them that you'd value their input; they will be flattered and, I'm sure, delighted to help.

Rule 6 – Be Clear on Who You Will Ask

Sometimes it feels easier to unburden ourselves to strangers; it's probably the feeling of being able to say what we need without fear of repercussions. The strong thread throughout this book, however, indicates that most people feel more comfortable sharing with their closest network.

I would recommend having a strong group of people whose opinion and discretion you trust and to whom you are comfortable turning when needed. I think we often know when we feel comfortable sharing with people.

I would recommend having a strong group of people whose opinion and discretion you trust.

Be selective about with whom you want to share and consider whether a relationship could be formalised. Don't underestimate the power of having a mentor, a mastermind group or a buddy. An individual or a group whose role is not just to support and advise but also to hold you accountable.

Unless it's formalised in a co-mentoring/buddy relationship, don't expect people to help you just because you have helped them or vice versa. Relationships don't need to be reciprocal; the support you give might come back from elsewhere in your network. It's the strength of the relationship and the knowledge that you or they are *willing* to help if called upon that's key.

And that relationship really is important. Growing relationships takes time. The deeper the relationship between you and your support network, the more they will want to help you and the better they will understand the type of advice that is right for you.

Don't rely just on relationships with people like you. We need to get out of our echo chambers and engage with opposing viewpoints.

Rule 7 – Seek People with Relevant Experience

Sourcing diverse opinions may help to expand the scope of the advice you receive, but identifying people who understand your challenge and who have personal experience of similar circumstances is invaluable.

Rule 8 – Take Counsel but Accept Responsibility

"You have got a team around you but you go in there and you're fighting on your own."

Billy Schwer was very clear about one thing when he spoke to me: take on board all the advice and experience you can gather but ultimately you're the one who has to live with the consequences of your decisions.

Other people will hold their opinions, often very strongly, about what you should do. It's good to listen and consider them carefully. At times advice from different people will contradict each other. That's fine, think of it as research. It's up to you to assess the pros and cons of the advice you receive and work out which route makes the most sense. Ultimately, it's your choice.

As Ivan Misner said, "You are the captain of your own ship. Every good captain needs the right crew around them but the responsibility for the ship's course lies with them."

Rule 9 – Look for the Positive

The nature of being in a position where you need to ask for help may well mean that you're predisposed to seeing a half-empty glass. However difficult it is, it will be much easier to find a solution if you change your perspective to one where the glass is half full.

It will be much easier to find a solution if you change your perspective to one where the glass is half full.

One of the most important rules of my mastermind sessions is that the person in the hot seat can only respond to any suggestion using two words: Thank you. That rule is there to prevent the instinctive response suggesting reasons why the proposed solution wouldn't work.

We often find it easier *not* to do something, becoming comfortable in our discomfort. Seeking positive solutions may require a mental shift and considerable effort but the payback can be huge.

We often find it easier not to do something, becoming comfortable in our discomfort.

If it helps, follow the advice that Andy Agathangelou (chapter 7) received and seek help for something you believe in rather than for you personally. If you're seeking success for a cause that's close to your heart, you'll find it easier to take tougher steps and engage others in the process.

Rule 10 – Help Others

'Blessed is he who gives without remembering and receives without forgetting.'

My favourite quote, by Elizabeth Asquith Bibesco, poet and daughter of the former British Prime Minister Lord Asquith, perfectly captures the winning philosophy when it comes to help and support.

I believe that everyone should have the opportunity to seek the support of others in achieving their goals but that doesn't mean that you sit back and wait for people to help you. Seek to help them first.

Let your network know that you are there for them, challenge them if you think they are struggling and don't always take no for an answer. Remember Ivan Misner's approach of 'Semantic Differential Questioning' in chapter 14? Ask them how they are, then when they say that they're OK, ask how they *really* are. Since my interview with Ivan I have naturally found myself using this technique, leading to some very powerful conversations.

But you have to mean it, back to that word 'authentic' again. I see people at networking events asking others automatically how they can help them in the first moments after meeting them. That doesn't feel real to me. Instead, truly engage with your network and look for opportunities to support them when it feels right.

Let go of the need to reciprocate when people help you; just accept their help graciously. Perhaps the opportunity to help them will come in the future; perhaps you will be able to pay it forward by helping someone else. Help should not be a quid pro quo, it should be in the moment.

Most importantly, when you help someone else, make it about them and not about you.

Most importantly, when you help someone else, make it about them and not about you.

What's Next?

I hope that you have enjoyed our journey together and you feel more comfortable and ready to turn to your network and request support. It will mean the world to me to hear how you get on. Please engage with me on the usual social networks, use the hashtag *#JustAskStories* to share your successes and your thoughts.

I'll be sharing some of those stories together with longer versions of interviews featured in this book, and other stories that we just haven't been able to squeeze in, on our website at *andylopata.com/justask*

So, join the conversation. You can also sign up to my three-weekly professional relationships tips newsletter *'Connecting is not Enough'* on the website.

If you would like to find out more about how vulnerable you are at the moment and where you can strengthen your approach, please visit andylopata.com/vulnerabilitywheel and download a free pdf of our diagnostic.

Finally, if you think this book can encourage someone else in your network to reach out and ask for the help they need, please pass on your copy, gift a copy or recommend it to them. Let's work together to encourage more people to *Just Ask*.

Acknowledgements

"If I have seen further it is by standing on the shoulders of giants."

Sir Isaac Newton

The famous quote from Sir Isaac Newton's 1676 letter to fellow scientist Robert Hooke could not be more appropriate to this venture.

I couldn't write a book encouraging you to let others help you without asking my own network for support. This has been a very different and much more difficult book to write compared to my previous publications. All of those were very much 'How to...' guides, with me putting my knowledge, ideas and expertise on paper. This book is much more about the people whose stories I've shared, whose expertise I've mined and whose support I've relied on.

So, there is a long list of people to thank, without whom (clichés aside) this book wouldn't have been possible.

First of all, I'd like to thank everyone who shared their stories with me. Unfortunately, I couldn't include all the stories or everything people shared because of space, so please visit *andylopata.com/justask* where I'll be adding new and unseen material.

I really appreciate the willingness of many people to open up, be truly vulnerable and share their stories. This involved leaving their egos to one side, something that is not for everyone.

The experts from around the world who shared their experience and perspectives and were also extremely generous with their time and support.

I used my own referrals techniques to secure some of the interviews, so I hugely appreciate the help of Gina Carr, Lesley Everett, Vanessa Vallely, Carole Spiers, Nigel Kershaw, Kelly Molson, Graham Webb, Grant Leboff and Sumiya Hemsi for valuable introductions. Also, Rob Skelton for mentioning Damian Hughes' work to me.

Thanks also to John and Johanna Jameson both for the pilot research project that accompanied this book and for their invaluable support. John has been a passionate supporter of this project and has shown a keen interest in the progress throughout the journey and his thoughtful advocacy is greatly appreciated. Johanna also contributed her insights as a counsellor alongside her role in the research project and encouragement. Lynda Shaw has also been a huge support and generous contributor to the book.

Jessica Wilson in Australia patiently transcribed many hours of interviews. Jess also gave me regular feedback that helped me to know that I was on the right track. Thanks also to my PA Natalie Finnigan, who during the period of researching and writing the early drafts persevered with scheduling and rescheduling interviews and managing to fit all of those calls and meetings alongside my day-to-day work.

My review circle of the original draft – Antoinette Dale Henderson, Rosie Slosek and my mum, Claire Lopata – were brilliant. They corrected my tired grammar, ruthlessly cut the flab from my writing, came up with great ideas and challenged me where needed.

I am hugely indebted to the editor of my last book, Liz Gooster, who helped me to craft my proposal and made the introduction to my original publisher so we could pique their interest in the first place. I am also very grateful to Mindy Gibbins-Klein, Emma Herbert, Alison Baugh, Philippa Hull and the team at Panoma Press, who showed faith when it was most needed!

I have had a huge amount of support from my network throughout the writing and rewriting process. I made the conscious decision to post my intention to write this book on Facebook when the idea first came up to ensure that friends held me accountable, and they have. In particular, David McQueen and Paul McGee have read chapters and given me encouraging feedback when I most needed it. David, along with Barbara Thompson, played a killer role in the final rewrite, really helping me to get this over the line.

Thanks to Christine Clacey, Tim Farazmand, Paul McGee (again!), Michael Roderick, Steven D'Souza and Lesley Everett and to my reviewers for draft three – Amanda Thurston, John Stapleton, Lee Warren and Davide Pagnotta. Thanks also to Carla Jones for being my sounding board on an impromptu writing retreat.

Finally, thank you. Thanks for reading this far. I hope that this book has meant something to you and can make a difference in your life.

If I can do anything for you, *Just Ask*.

Endnotes

1   William and Harry in Their Own Words. CalmZine, 25 April 2017

2   https://www.ted.com/talks/brene_brown_on_vulnerability?language=en

3   *S.U.M.O. (Shut Up Move On)*. McGee, P. Capstone Publishing, 2005, 2001

4   www.landmarkworldwide.com

5   Possibly referring to Leonard Cohen's 'Anthem': "There is a crack, a crack in everything. That's how the light gets in."

6   *The Truth about Trust in Business: How to Enrich the Bottom Line, Improve Retention, and Build Valuable Relationships for Success.* Hall, V. Emerald Book Company, July 2009

7   *Healing Begins in the Kitchen.* Misner, I. & Misner, B. Esposito Eddie, En Passant Publishing, 2017

8   *Think and Grow Rich.* Hill, N. 1938. The full chapter on Masterminding can be read here: http://www.sacred-texts.com/nth/tgr/tgr15.htm

9   *The Start-up of You: Adapt to the Future, Invest in Yourself and Transform your Career.* Hoffman, R., Random House Business Books, 2013

10   https://www.chathamhouse.org/about-us/chatham-house-rule

11   *Mitigating Malicious Envy: Why Successful Individuals Should Reveal Their Failures.* Abi-Esber, N., Hall, B., Buell, R. W. & Huang, L., Journal of Experimental Psychology: General, 2019

12   *Rio Ferdinand: My generation killed the England football team.* Wilson, R., *The Times,* 12 May 2018

13   *How the Psychology of the England Football Team Could Change Your Life.* Saner, E., *The Guardian,* 10 July 2018

14   *The Barcelona Way: How to Create a High-Performance Culture.* Hughes, D., Macmillan, August 2018

15   Michelle Obama, *The Late Show* with Stephen Colbert, 30 November 2018

16   Margaret Thatcher, Conservative Party Conference, 10 October 1980

17   Are the Tories Losing Ground or Regaining It? YouGov poll, 25 May 2017

18   Matt Hancock, *The Andrew Marr Show.* BBC1, 15 March 2020

19   John McDonnell: 'I Can't Forgive Tories.' BBC News, 21 November 2018

20   https://www.bbc.co.uk/news/world-us-canada-53521143

21   *Equal Power.* Swinson, J., Atlantic Books, 2018

22   British politician assassinated in June 2016

23   *What Happened.* Clinton, H. R., Simon and Schuster, September 2017

24   *Who is in your Personal Boardroom?* King, Z. & Scott, A., Personal Boardroom Ltd, 2014

25   *Why Are the Youth the Loneliest Generation?* Sondhelm, R., Titford, B., Scahill, T., Rumble, L., Tjia, O., Nead, S. & Parkyn, E., University of Birmingham Undergraduate Study, January 2019

26   *An Investigation of Loneliness and Perfectionism in University Students.* Arslan, C. & Özyesil, Z., Procedia – Social and Behavioral Sciences, 2010

27   *The Secrets of Long Life.* Buettner D., *National Geographic Magazine,* November 2005

About the Author

A specialist in professional relationships and networking for over 20 years, Andy Lopata was called 'one of Europe's leading business networking strategists' by the *Financial Times* and 'a true master of networking' by *The Independent* and Forbes.com.

A very experienced international speaker, Andy is the author of five books, has been quoted in a number of other business books and regularly quoted in the international press.

Andy is a Fellow and a board member of the Professional Speaking Association UK & Ireland (PSA) and a Fellow of the Learning and Performance Institute as well as a Master of the Institute for Sales Management. He is also one of just 26 recipients of the PSA's top honour, the Award of Excellence.

My Black Dog Charity

A percentage of royalties from each sale of this book are being donated to My Black Dog.

My Black Dog is a peer to peer online support service for people struggling with their mental health in England and Wales. All of our volunteers have grappled with their own black dogs and understand what you are going through. We are online every day and you can talk to us through an online chat function on the website. **When you don't know who to talk to, talk to someone who gets it.**

www.myblackdog.co

Registered Charity Number 1182690

Also available by Andy Lopata:

The Connected Leadership Podcast

Presented by
Andy Lopata

Professional relationships strategist and author of *Connected Leadership* Andy Lopata is joined by guests from business leaders, through subject matter experts to sports stars and more as they discuss the role that networks and professional relationships play in leadership success.

The perfect listen for business leaders and those aspiring to leadership positions, Andy and his guests discuss key topics relevant to career and leadership success including: mentoring, managing teams, the power of storytelling and communicating effectively to develop relationships, vulnerability and asking for help, how technology impacts leadership, scaling businesses and much more.

Each week two episodes are published. On Mondays there is a full interview and then on Thursday Andy's guests share their own relationship stories and favourite resources in a shorter episode.

Once a month, Andy is joined by Italian leadership expert Luca Signoretti, to discuss different approaches to developing professional relationships for business leaders.

Available on Apple Podcasts, Amazon podcasts, Stitcher, Spotify and all major podcast channels.

https://podfollow.com/connectedleadership/

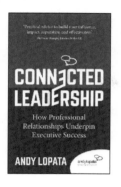

Connected Leadership

How Professional
Relationships Underpin
Executive Success

Andy Lopata

"Practical advice to build your influence, impact, reputation and effectiveness"

Phil Jones MBE, Managing Director, Brother UK

Professional Relationships Matter

You can often tell the quality of a leader not just from the calibre of his or her relationships, but by the ease with which they draw on them and the speed and willingness with which people respond.

Professional relationships lie at the heart of executive success. Despite this, many leaders leave their professional relationships to chance and actively discourage their staff from forming strong bonds.

In this new book professional relationships expert Andy Lopata explores just how important strong relationships are and how to build a supportive network.

"Andy is one of the pre-eminent experts of his generation, his new book is a comprehensive and welcome summary of his thinking."

Tim Farazmand, Former Chairman, British Private Equity & Venture Capital Association

First published in 2020 by Panoma Press Ltd   9781784529147

Recommended

How to sell through
networking and referrals

Andy Lopata

Referrals and recommendations are the most effective drivers of new business. This book will show you how to make your business thrive by generating referrals and sales from your own networks cheaply, effectively and quickly.

You will discover:

- How to generate more of the leads that produce better quality business, leads that convert more easily and more quickly into real sales

- Detailed guidance on how to use LinkedIn to generate referrals

- Practical, takeaway information which can be implemented easily in any business that needs to generate new sales

"Should be a mandatory read for anyone pursuing a career in sales and marketing-related fields."

Colin Wright, Senior Vice-President, Global Sales Development, MasterCard

"Powerful referrals are the foundation for any successful business and this is a practical guide to both receiving and giving high quality introductions."

Nigel Kershaw OBE, CEO, Big Issue Invest and Group Chairman, The Big Issue Company Ltd

First published in 2011 by Financial Times Prentice Hall   9780273757962

...and death came third!

The Definitive Guide to Networking and Speaking in Public

Andy Lopata and Peter Roper

- Do you dread going to networking events?

- Do you hide at the back of the room when you have the opportunity to present your business?

In 1984 a New York Times Survey on Social Anxiety placed death third in the list of people's biggest fears. The top two responses were walking into a room full of strangers and speaking in public.

Facing these two fears head on, *...and death came third!* rocketed straight to Number Two on the Amazon UK bestseller lists on publication of its First Edition in 2006. Since then thousands of people have turned to its pages to help them network and present with much more confidence.

"Powerful, practical advice on both cultivating great networking relationships and speaking with confidence: two skills of vital importance to today's successful business person."

**Bob Burg, Author, *Endless Referrals:
Network Your Everyday Contacts Into Sales***

"A must read for anyone who wants to get on in business."

**Lord Digby Jones, Former Director-General of the CBI
and Minister of State for Trade**

Second edition published in 2011 by Ecademy Press   9781907722301

Index

Unilever 163, 165

trust 57

women 197, 206, 208–9

wallowing 7–8, 19

Weafer, Sean 134

Webb, Hattie 23–4, 52–3, 144

wellbeing 167

see also mental health

wheelchair rugby 81, 100

William, Prince 6

willingness to accept help 86–7

women 197, 203–4, 206–11

Wong, Ricky 167–8

Woodward, Clive 173–4, 176–7, 187–8

Wright, Colin 185–6

younger generations 219–24

Zimbabwe 228